The American Dream!
Building Your Home and Wealth!

A Step by Step Custom Home Design Guide
Design Smart! Lower Costs and Improve Appraisals
From a Custom Builder's Perspective

Architectural Design by Ramses Buena

BY:

Steven M. Washburn, President
Washburn Custom Builders
SAHBA Certified Custom Builder
www.WashburnBuilders.com

ISBN: 1-4107-2632-0 (E-book)
ISBN: 1-4107-2631-2 (Paperback)

This book is printed on acid free paper.

1st Books - rev. 06/11/04

A MUST READ FOR ANYONE THINKING OF DESIGNING, BUYING, BUILDING, OR SELLING A HOME!

"Washburn Builders exemplify the high standards of quality, craftsmanship, reliability, and experience as a SAHBA Certified Custom Builder."
Roger Yohem, SAHBA Communications Director

"Bravo, I'll refer all of my clients to your book. It's the perfect book for those who have ever even remotely thought of building a home."
Lucy Barraza, RE/MAX Premier Realty

"Working with a custom home contractor <Washburn> was an exciting and enjoyable experience. We would recommend building a custom home to anyone."
Cristal and German Bojorquez

TABLE OF CONTENTS

HOW THIS BOOK CAN HELP YOU

If you have picked this book up, you are likely choosing a publication to help you better understand the **design and building process** for your **dream home**. If this is the case, then you will want to learn both what to do, and more importantly what not to do, so you can maximize your home design and building experience while avoiding the many potential mistakes that we often hear about during the construction process. Also, you are likely entering into this endeavor with a significant other, and you will want to reduce the stress of the process as much as possible. The stories of break-up are legendary while experiencing the emotion charged issues surrounding the designing and building of your **dream home**.

So how can this book help? Our experience in successfully designing and building homes, for often demanding custom home clients, has given us a unique perspective on what it takes to succeed in the design and building process while still maintaining your sanity. One of our recent clients commented that we **"made building their home easy"**, which in turn helped keep both husband and wife relatively stress free. Personalities differ for sure, but we have found that **understanding the process and expectations can greatly reduce the anxiety that can be associated with the process**. Take the time to buy and read this book together, and you will understand much more about the process, and therefore be able to come together on basic decisions affecting your dream home.

When you are through, please provide us with feedback as to how this book may have helped you in your process.

Steven M. Washburn

DEDICATIONS

I must start any of my efforts with a huge thank you to God for all of my blessings and success throughout my life. I must also thank my wife Jeanette and family for their support and tolerance of my often focused efforts, which meant frequently working from very early in the morning to "too late" in the evening. Thank you all for your patience and sacrifices.

The origin of this series of books is simply a response to the many Q & A sessions that occurred with my clients, associates and sub-contractors over many years, along with my experience in handling various issues encountered on actual construction projects. There are endless issues that were discussed, and numerous ways to solve specific concerns which arise during the design and construction of various projects. It is these brain storming and Q & A meetings that provided the information contained in these books. The common thread that each client contributed was the need and desire to obtain answers to questions that affect the design, quality, timing and cost of their project. The basic nature of answering these questions could be a very dry read, so I have chosen a look-up friendly format to allow for easy use as a reference tool during the course of a project, which reflects the process of discovery during design and construction. The issues discussed never surfaced all at once, but developed and became apparent as they became important and pertinent to the work and choices at hand.

I offer a special thanks to each and every client, associate and sub-contractor, which I had the privilege of working, those who helped me answer these questions for myself and my clients. The contribution list is extensive, and I am not sure I will include every individual who provided contributions to this book, although I will try both here and in the references at the back of this book. Success and failure are both excellent tools for learning, and I attempted, over the years, to use other peoples' failures as learning tools, so that I could avoid these very same mistakes. I will simply thank these individuals and organizations as a group, because they taught me much about what not to do! On the other hand, I will specifically name some people and organizations that have helped me grow as a builder, and therefore helped in the success of my client's projects: Jim Pitts and his entire staff at Design Solutions provided endless expertise and professionalism in preparing excellent sets of working drawings that have been the basis for many of my projects, learning new code details as they occurred, and helping each client develop a creative and intelligent design for their home has been an invaluable tool in my own personal learning process. Also, I need to thank all of my previous employers and hands-on teachers from Apache Construction Company in 1973, to my brother Gerard's order of 4000 slump block to my backyard as a young adult with the statement "we are going to teach you to lay block" and he did! In addition, My sources at the back of this book provide a long list of excellent sub-contractors who have helped teach me what excellence in their respective trades means to an overall project. I have often deferred to their expertise to make key decisions that have helped make a project an outstanding example of what it could be, rather than just another average project. Finally, I would like to thank Dr. Robert A. Clark and Gavin Fielding, of the University of Arizona Hydrology and Water Resources Department, for taking the time and effort to teach me valuable information concerning the environmental impact of construction and development. Their efforts have had, and continue to have, positive contributions in the water and environmental challenges we are facing in the coming years, through both the committees I serve on and my own construction projects and consultations with clients. To all of these individuals and organizations I say thank you for your contributions to this series of books.

WHAT THIS BOOK IS, AND WHAT IT IS NOT

A brief discussion of what this series of books is, and what it is not, is in order, and included in each of our publications. It would be presumptuous of us to assume we know all there is to know about design and building. The value we offer is in sharing our experience with interested consumers with the intent of helping them better understand the process we work with on a day-to-day basis.

Our series of books is designed to focus on our part in the process, which can be compared to the coach of a sports team and his/her team captains. It is our job, and responsibility, to help clients accomplish their goal of designing and building their dream home successfully by pulling together a skilled team of professionals and managing them according to our client's wishes. With this in mind, we focus on the process as it affects this goal and the client. Full exploration of the design and building process would require volumes of books and years of study, which we believe is not the intent of a client. Typically you do not want to become builders, engineers, hydrologists, architects, or any of the other experts required to help you design and build your project. However, you would generally want to understand the process, time frame, and financial impact of your decisions.

INTRODUCTION

This publication is an offshoot of our first book Designing and Building Custom Homes and Your Wealth, From a Custom Builders Perspective. Our first publication was intended to provide a simple primer of the basic process and motivation for pursuing the goal of designing and building your dream home. This book will take you through the designing thought process, from a custom builder's perspective, in a sequential format. It should be noted that we are design builders, not architects or engineers. The design builder often depends on engineers and architects to pull their projects together into a completed set of plans for permitting and building purposes. The builder's expertise is in providing direction to these professionals based on site analysis and design directives to accomplish the goals of the client. These goals often involve balancing the cost of the project with the desire to build a beautiful home of high quality on a budget. Owners, architects and engineers rely on the builder to make this happen, while we as builders rely on these professionals to pull our field designs together into a complete set of plans and specifications. In short, you as a client want the biggest bang for the buck, and your builder is charged with the responsibility of helping you accomplish that goal.

Your expectations in this process are very likely going to have a major impact on both your stress level and overall satisfaction when you are finished. The process often ranges from a few months to a year to complete, and you will deal with many decisions involving many thousands of dollars, which you often cannot easily change after they are made. Taking the time to understand the process and adjust your expectations is critical to your happiness during the process. It is our hope that this publication will help you accomplish both of these objectives, and therefore help make your experience much more fun and enjoyable.

CHAPTER 1

This chapter provides information concerning some of the basic issues you will want to review prior to beginning your site selection and design process. They include varied subject matter with brief discussions on each, which are designed to increase your awareness, help focus your efforts, and reduce the possibility of costly mistakes.

OBJECTIVES AND GOALS

The main objective of the design and building process is to create an interior and exterior environment for your family to live in and conduct daily activities. A secondary goal (primary for some) is to build in value to help enhance the owner's net worth through equity in the property. The primary objective is a very large and wide open subject that can take many forms. Historically architects from Spain's Antonio Gaudi to America's Frank Lloyd Wright have designed projects ranging from fantasy in the case of Gaudi's Sacred Family Cathedral in Barcelona, to Wright's sparsely designed and furnished homes we see in the publication about Wright's works called "A Retrospective View" (Copplestone 2001). While these are two extreme examples, the following is an exercise designed to help you define your architectural focus.

I suggest subscribing to, and tearing pages from, your favorite architectural magazines to help you better define the design and environments you like. The process of tearing out pages of interiors and exteriors that are pleasing to you will give both you and your builder/architect direction. The design process should be a synergistic effort between owner, builder, and architect, and result in a creation that reflects the owners wishes, the knowledge and experience of the builder and architect, and remains focused on meeting the budget constraints of the client.

Our past clients have arrived with many styles and designs of architecture that they felt were very confusing in the beginning. However, these tears provide valuable information to help you communicate what types of environments appeal to your tastes and feelings. One of my recent clients said that as a child she always liked reading a book while looking through a particular style of window while the fireplace was burning alongside her. This was an extremely important feeling for her, and so we designed the window and door openings, fireplace, view orientation (for light and view), as well as the ceiling height and back patio to meet this "feeling".

I should step back a moment and recognize that not everyone will be designing their **dream home** from scratch. However, even in existing plans you will often have the opportunity to determine site orientation, window size changes, and other pre-construction alterations that can help you accomplish personalized touches. Some builders may not be set up for a lot of changes, but they are usually willing to accommodate some customized features to make a sale. Also, be sure to listen to their feedback to avoid potential mistakes. There are times we have counseled against certain choices, with sound supporting reasoning that is easily understood when it is explained. In other words, depend on your hired professional to guide you through the decision making process, but be sure you have supporting information so the decision is yours in the end.

No matter if your tastes embrace the fantasy of Antonio Gaudi, the horizontal lines of Frank Lloyd Wright, or the homes you see in your own city, it is a great idea to begin any design process with a few weeks of tearing photos and starting your own "wish list" file. Once you have defined your likes and dislikes, you should begin looking for your builder and designer/architect. (see: Your architect, designer, & builder choices)

YOUR ARCHITECT, DESIGNER, & BUILDER CHOICES

CHOOSING A DESIGNER OR ARCHITECT

Designers are not architects, but they are often excellent choices for the design of your home, and may save you significant amount of expense on your project, if it does not require the services of an architect. Architects are often needed when a design objective, or project restriction, specifies the services of a licensed architect. This often occurs when the owner's desire is for a more elaborate and creative project, or when either the home owner's association or building services of the local area require an architectural stamp on the plans.

Designers and Architects are skilled professionals, and both have a place in the building industry. Ask your builder for designer or architect recommendations, and I encourage you to bring your builder on board prior to the start of design! The synergy of owner, designer and builder is a powerful combination that will help you in numerous ways. The design will be much better because the designer and builder have skills and talents that are specific and unique to each of their fields, and you will want to have them discuss your project's design details to be sure your plans reflect the most intelligent method of building and the use of the current construction materials and methods. Your designer or architect is the creative type, while your builder must actually build the ideas on paper and make them reality. Plus, you will want to be closely involved in this process to be sure your specific needs and wants are incorporated into the plans. Usually your builder will be willing to work on a retainer during this phase, which can be negotiated as part of his/her entire contractor's fee, so it is not likely that the additional service will cost you more money, but actually reduce your expense since you will avoid including many mistakes in your plans.

UTILITIES

BE SURE OF THE UTILITIES ON YOUR BUILDING SITE

This sounds like a simple question, but is often overlooked during the land purchase process. Many sites do not have natural gas lines, municipal water is not always available, electricity is not always close to the site and municipal sewer connections are also not a given. Ask your builder and realtor to help you answer all of the above utility questions prior to buying your land!

I have often consulted with clients on sites that have difficult and expensive sewage system requirements, no natural gas availability, water wells that are not producing sufficient water for their home, and electricity that costs thousands of dollars to extend to the building site, not to mention phone and cable T V issues. Do a little home work here and save yourself both grief and dollars later!

SEWAGE SYSTEM

CHECK THE TYPE OF SEWAGE DISPOSAL SYSTEM YOU WILL NEED, AND FIND OUT WHAT IT WILL COST

Usually a simple check to see if you have a municipal sewer connection is sufficient. If there is not a sewer connection, then you will need to be sure your soil drains well, which involves a percolation test, and should be handled by your builder or realtor. Be sure the percolation test is performed in the area you expect to place your septic system, and I recommend a licensed engineer for the design of the system, as well as the supervision of the actual test. (Nichols)

There are sites that do not drain well, usually due to clay or rock conditions. If the soil drains too slow or too fast, then the engineer will design the system to adjust for the conditions. This may include an expensive alternative system, and you will want to know the possibility of this extra expense prior to buying the land. Yes, you will spend some up-front money here, but it is essential to know the potential conditions for your future sewage system, as you must have a sewer connection, and **it is a good idea to know how it should be designed, where it should be located and how much it is likely to cost.** (Nichols)

BUYING PLANS FROM A PLAN SERVICE

You have most likely seen plan books at the grocery store check-out counter, blue print supply services and in book stores. These plan books can be valuable tools in defining what you like, and most importantly, what you do not like in a floor plan and exterior elevation (how the house will look). I recommend looking through a few of these books prior to meeting with your designer and builder, so that you have a good idea what size, style and traffic flow pattern you prefer. Also, I recommend looking through Architectural Digest, your local home and garden magazines, and any decorator publications that you find that can help you define the atmosphere you want to experience when actually living in your new home. Tear out pages you like and keep them in a file to review with your builder and architect.

Should you actually buy a set of plans from one of these plan book companies? Usually I say no! Why? Because you will need to hire professional services to add much more to the set of plans in order to actually obtain a permit, and you will likely save very little money in addition to limiting floor plan and design changes that are likely to be suggested to customize your home to meet your own needs and wants. Also, building a home that anyone else can build by buying this same set of plans from the plan book will not help your individual custom home appraisal in the end. Most appraisers know a cookie cutter type model when they see it, and it is likely to reduce your appraised value. Use the ideas these resources offer, but enlist the services of a professional to create your own unique design.

USING AN EXISTING SET OF PLANS

Once you have a good idea of what you want, you may ask your builder if he/she has some existing plans that could be modified to meet your needs. This could reduce both time and the expense of producing a full set of new plans. There is often no need to re-invent the wheel, if your tastes are similar to some of the builder's work you like.

One note of caution. Be sure the plans are up-to-date with respect to current codes, as there have been significant changes that will likely affect older sets of plans, even though they have been previously approved.

ABOUT DESIGN BUILDERS

Design builders are usually set up to serve clients more quickly and efficiently than fragmenting the process, and hiring each individual professional separately. They tend to be in the building planning and design activity on a daily basis, and you will most likely experience a "one stop" shopping situation, which can reduce your time and work and thus eventually help you reduce stress. Be sure you check out the reputation of the builder, visit his/her projects, and talk to some of his past clients. Many times a design builder can be your best option for controlling costs too, due to the fact that they are up-to-date with regard to current costs of materials and services that you may want to use in your project. Masonry, steel, alternative material or frame for the exterior? What are the costs of tile, granite, plumbing fixtures, cabinet choices, lighting fixtures, fireplaces and other choices in the interior?

WHEN SHOULD I CHOOSE A BUILDER?

You and your builder will be spending a great deal of time together dealing with often emotion charged issues of the design and construction of your home. It is very important that your personalities work well together, that he/she has the experience and resources required to complete your home, that you trust him/her with decisions, and that you feel he/she has integrity in dealing with your project.

It is best to choose a builder as early in your project as possible. His/her input can help you select the best building site, design your project with cost savings and value engineering in mind, help you choose certain materials and components for your project, and generally set the stage for a more controlled and smooth building experience. His/her early involvement will often result in little or no overall cost increase, and most often results in reductions of overall costs, especially if you handle his/her up-front consulting fees in the way I suggest in the contractual part of this publication. I cannot overstate the importance of selecting an experienced team of professionals that know how to deal with your project's demands. Your builder is key to a successful experience, and early selection of a builder that you can work with is very important. I suggest asking for referrals in your area, including your local builder's association, and then selecting three potential builders for an interview. Prepare a list of questions that are important to your decision making process, schedule an appointment to meet your builder for an interview, and ask to tour some of his/her completed and current projects, so you can see his/her work first hand.

SCHEDULE EXPECTATIONS

There are two schedules on a typical project. The first is for the development and production of your design and working drawings, and securing a building permit along with the approval of any HOA Architectural Committee. The second is for the actual construction of your home.

Depending on the speed of your floor plan selection, and the conditions present on your building site, completing the design, working drawings, and permitting of your home can range from a few weeks to a few months. There are now approvals required for many additional issues in most regions of the country. We often see approvals for hillside development, plant preservation, wildlife impact, grading and drainage restrictions, architectural restrictions, zoning, as well as the typical building structural review process. There are times it seems like the project will never start, but time spent in the preparation of a good set of plans is essential to assuring the smooth progression of the entire project!

The actual custom home construction schedule typically ranges from seven to twelve months, depending upon site conditions, size of the home, and materials & finishes selected for the project. We have built 3600 square foot homes (6000 square foot under roof) in less than six months, while some more complex homes with numerous customer changes can run closer to nine months or more. However, a typical schedule runs from six to seven months. Be sure to ask for a specific schedule, so you will know when key issues need your input and choices.

THE PAYOFF

What is the end payoff and why is it worth the hassle? We have successfully designed and built medium and large custom homes for clients in the time frame of seven to eleven months (building time) with equity positions ranging from $50,000 to $400,000 from the time that they moved into their homes. **I believe strongly that the builder and architect/designer are much more successful if they can help their client accomplish their own goals, both for their home and their equity in their property.**

There are specific keys to achieving this goal, which we discuss in our **What the Smart Money Already Knows** book (Washburn 2002). The larger and more complex the project the longer it takes, but often more equity is involved. The process is work to be sure, but the payoff is frequently substantially more equity than you would have if you simply purchased an existing home. The extra equity is achieved by approaching your project from a well informed and systematic stand point, and including three important professionals, your builder, realtor, and designer/architect. These three professionals can help stack the deck in your favor and keep you on track towards the best chance of a successful payoff in the end. A beautiful and high quality home that reflects your wants and needs, along with substantial equity from the time you turn the key.

CHAPTER 2

THE DESIGN PROCESS Basic STEPS TO ARCHITECTURAL DESIGNING

WISH LIST

It is best to start defining your **Dream Home** by starting a structured wish list of important items you would like to see incorporated into your home design. This is likely to include style, number of bedrooms, bathrooms, formal or informal architectural style, great room or traditional living area, formal dining room, fireplaces, entertainment areas, an many other items that are unique to your family's lifestyle and needs. (see index)

Designing your custom home involves sequential steps which are defined as follows:

Reminder: These steps are from a builder's perspective and would likely be different if listed from either an architect or engineer's perspective.

Step #1 Floor plan and site analysis

This step is the foundation page for all other pages, so it must be carefully prepared and verified **before** moving ahead to any other step. Changes after moving on to the following steps will involve multiple page changes, and therefore increase the time and cost of the design process. Take sufficient time to mentally live in your floor plan to be sure you can envision your traffic flow, room uses, and lifestyle. (see site topography section)

11

Step #2 Exterior elevations

After your floor plan is set you will move on to the exterior elevations, or how your home will look from the outside (curb appeal). This is where you get to express yourself in architectural style and personality. Mediterranean, Santa Fe, Spanish Colonial, Contemporary or many other architectural choices.

Now is the time for preliminary submittal of your project to your Home Owners Association Architectural Committee, if you have one. **Do not proceed to step #3 until you have your HOA approval for your site plan, floor plan and elevations!**

Step #3 Interior elevations and ceiling heights

Here is where you select how your interior is going to feel. Lower ceilings in smaller rooms provide more intimate feeling while higher ceilings in larger (usually main living areas) will provide a more grand and open feeling. Also, use of varied building material textures and colors are often explored as a large component of creating the inside atmosphere of your home.

Step #4 Specification choices

There is a long list of specification choices you will need to choose from in this process. Heating and Air Conditioning, plumbing and light fixtures, tile, cabinets, doors, windows, paint, counter tops, shower and tub enclosures, granite and many more items specific to your project. Also, this is the step where you will most impact your cost of construction (Budget). A quick review of our discussion on these issues is definitely in order, if you want to keep control of your budget!

Step #5 Check set

Your builder and architect/designer should provide you with a final check set of working drawings for your home. You do not need to be a builder to understand these, only have a builder willing to explain any issues you do not understand. You will want to focus on the floor plan, elevations, plumbing, electrical and interior elevations for the most part. Most of the work should have already been included in the plans, though there are often details that may have been left out. **Be sure these are in your plan to avoid potential Change Orders to add them later! Unnecessary** Change Orders should be avoided whenever possible, as they often result in extra expense to you!

Step #6 Permit and HOA final submittals

Your builder and architect/designer should now incorporate your check set notes, engineering notes, and any HOA required alterations into your working drawings for final submittal for permitting and final HOA approval. This often includes a separate landscape plan to satisfy both the HOA and the regulatory entity. At this point you should also provide necessary documents to your lender to complete your financing, if you plan to use a lender.

A MORE DETAILED LOOK OF EACH STEP

The following information is an outline of the issues, which is intended to provide you with basic design structure, so that you will be aware of what each basic task involves. We explore these issues to accomplish the goals of **Designing Smart! Lowering Costs and Improving Appraisals,** which in turn will provide you a structured track to guide you through the process. Basic design knowledge will be sufficient for most readers, and it is my intent to keep the discussion brief and to the point with regard to the following topics. Each topic has an impact on both your design and budget, but we will focus only on the information required for you to make your decision with regard to your home. More detailed discussions may be necessary at times, depending upon your own unique building site or design situation, and these should be discussed with your builder and/or architect as these issues present themselves.

STEP ONE DETAIL

You may note that the step one detail involves much more information than any other part of this publication. The reasons will become evident as you explore them. Please note that all of these issues may not apply to your individual project, however, you should at least be aware that they exist, and how they may impact design, construction planning, and execution on your building site. **I cannot over emphasize the need to become familiar with these issues, and to use your builder, designer/architect and engineers to completely deal with this phase to avoid potential problems!**

Site topography, soil type, VIEWS, and exposure to the Sun are the issues you will want to focus on from the very start. This is where the synergy of your builder, designer, and you will begin. I suggest working a little backwards in the respect that I feel you should take your end budget and work backwards. What do I mean? Well your end objective is to finish with a unique custom home that is both livable for your family and a good investment. To accomplish these goals you will need to start with your end budget in mind, and ask your builder and designer to help you design within this constraint. This must be communicated from the very start, as your initial decisions involve defining your floor plan, view orientation and site location related to topography, and will play a critical part in your budgeting success. Also, you will want to plan for the best sun exposure orientation, which impacts the energy efficiency and livability of your home.

For example, your views may be to the Northeast and West, which means you will need to contend with the hot afternoon sun on the West side of your home. You will want to enjoy the view with windows, but not endure the sunshine and heat which can fade fabric and increase your cooling bills.

In this case your designer/architect and builder will likely suggest that you add patio roofing on the West side of your design, while on the Northeast side you may require less roofing cover. In addition, you may choose to orient the back of your home to the Northeast, which will also allow for additional shade in the afternoon hours. Be sure to ask questions and fully explore site selection with your builder and designer/architect, as you do not get a second chance to place your home!

TOPOGRAPHY

ABOUT THE TOPOGRAPHY OF YOUR POTENTIAL BUILDING SITE

What is topography? Simply stated, it is the slope contour of your land. How steep it is, and where will you want to situate your home? Builders, designers/architects, engineers and building code officials use a topography map "Topo Map", which typically show continuous lines at each elevation change on your building site (usually at intervals of 1 to 2 feet for design purposes). Topography conditions are important on your site because you want to be sure your home will actually fit on the site, be placed where you want it, and not increase your building costs unnecessarily due to expensive retainer and restrainer walls, often required on hillside building sites (Pitts).

If you have hired a builder by now, ask him/her to study your topography map and visit your site for a basic analysis. This is usually a simple process that takes less than a day, and will help assure you that you will be able to achieve the size and style home you desire. Also, ask your builder to review the utilities, drainage and soils type, to the extent possible, during this visit, to be sure you have a good idea how these issues will impact your project. (see utilities and soils part of this publication)

15

To help keep building costs down a good rule of thumb is to simply try to choose a building site that is not too steep or hilly and consists of mostly soil rather than rock. That being said, we often build on steep hillsides because clients and buyers like the dramatic look and feel of well designed homes on the tops and sides of hills. Also, these can often be associated with rock, which will definitely require a builder familiar with the conditions and demands of this type project. Finally, square pegs can be put into round holes, homes on hillsides and rock, but there are costs associated with this type of construction, and you should factor these into your budgeting formula.

Here is an excellent example of an extremely difficult site that required careful planning and execution. Fortunately we did not encounter solid rock conditions, but the site ranged between 15% and 25% slopes, and the owner needed to meet a budget to begin the project. We selected a combination of retainer walls, rip-rap slopes, and cut & fill (engineered compaction) to meet the demands of this site. (see below)

Architectural Design by Ollanik Company

Here is the successful result of our efforts! A one level 2800 square foot home with a step down garage. We altered the original Ollanik design by changing the tall rear stem walls to a yard retainer wall system that allowed for the addition of a back yard rather than a sharp drop in elevation. This reduced costs and added to the overall design. The front retainer wall was also re-configured to improve drainage control and enhance the front entry area. (see below)

Note the alternative site placement on this building site, which improves both views and sun exposure. The entrance design will be enhanced further by incorporating a court yard entry double gate/door, which will lead from the garage (at the left of this photo) to the front door. Also note the water control (rain run-off) provided by the water proofed front retainer wall (with French drains).

SITE-PLAN AND ORIENTATION

It is time to think outside the box! I have often seen the regimented lay-out of a subdivision with every home facing directly towards the street, totally ignoring the views and sun exposure! This may be a necessity in tract home sub-divisions, but it is often not required in semi-custom and custom home neighborhoods. A complete analysis of your building site topography, water drainage, soils, view orientation, and sun exposure is in order, at the very least.

We routinely turn homes in many different directions to accomplish the best view and sun exposure, and we highly recommend that you think outside the box when orienting your own home placement. Our past projects that fall in this non-traditional site orientation category have set the standards for appraisal in their respective neighborhoods. One such home sold for over 30% more than any home that had previously sold on the street where it was located. On the other hand, a home directly across the street from one these (built by another builder) sat empty for over a year. The other builder oriented his project square with the street and missed the chance to take advantage of the beautiful mountain views that a simple turn of his house would have accomplished. Homes all around this one sold, in large part due to this oversight. It is wise to explore all of your site possibilities.

Non traditional orientation requires a builder, realtor, and architect/designer with the skill and experience to know what will work from both a buildable and sellable standpoint. Be sure you consult experienced professionals to accomplish this task (Pitts).

Architectural Design by Design Solutions (Jim Pitts)

This 4000 square foot (heated and cooled) home is a perfect example of alternative site plan placement. The back of the home facing the street while the front entry views are towards a mountain. (see view below) This is the side view, which shows the radius entry to the right of the garage, and will include guest parking and an entry patio announcing to guests where the front door is located. Hardscape, parking placement, and landscape design are especially important for this type of placement. They announce your entry, and guide traffic flow where you want it, while keeping the traffic flow away from areas that are to remain private.

Back patio view of the same home, which faces the road.
Foundation by Scott Abernathy Concrete

This home was placed on nearly solid rock conditions after months of architectural design and site analysis involving the builder, architects and foundation sub-contractor. The strategy employed a combination of restrainer walls, which you see below the patio here, retainer walls on the upper side of the hill, and some removal of on-site rock. The strategy needed to handle site water drainage and dramatically reduce the disturbance to the surrounding natural desert. See the photo below for a view of the cut into the rock hill.

Note the minimal cut required at right. Special water drainage control efforts were employed to reduce the need to remove rock outside of the building envelope. The result allows the home to appear as though it was set down on the building pad, rather than bull dozed into the hill. (grading by Salazar excavation Co)

SITE GRADING PLAN AND SITE WALLS (IF NEEDED)

Site preparation will be guided by the style, size and configuration of your home (Pitts). Some home sites will require a grading process called cut and fill, while some will employ site walls and fill, and others will need pillars and floor joists, or there may be a combination of these. What does this mean to the client? Simply that any one of these choices **will** have an impact on your budget, so you will want to understand what is happening on your site, and how each of the choices affect the budget. You will want to be sure your builder and designer/architect are skilled in dealing with sites like yours, and fully discuss the potential strategies unique to your site.

Our past projects have involved solid rock on steep slopes (over 15%) with the need to install substantial retainer and restrainer walls. There are a number of strategies a builder can use to successfully deal with slope and rock issues. Some include design, others include choices of materials, while still others involve building location. It is most important that you understand the complexity and importance of this issue, and be sure you hire a professional capable of handling the unique demands of this task. (see discussion on soil types)

Your builder's strategy in dealing with these issues should come from experience! This is no time for on the job training at your expense!

ALTERNATIVE FOUNDATION OPTIONS, POST TENSION, TRADITIONAL FOOTERS, STEM-WALLS AND SLABS, COLUMNS AND FLOOR JOISTS

Many of my clients ask about various types of foundations that they have heard and read about. Typically it is best to look carefully at the soils conditions and type of building you are constructing, and then consult with the soils and structural engineers to design the correct type of foundation for your site and design. The answer may be post tension, footer & stem wall, or a host of other choices that the engineers suggest. (Pitts) (Grenier)

I often suggest going with the flow as related to the topography of the land, and using the slopes to your advantage, instead of fighting against the reality of the building site. What this usually involves is using a slope to help create part of your floor plan in the traffic flow pattern that is of most help to your floor plan goals. For example, if you have a steep slope on your building site, and you must build in this area of the lot for one reason or another, then you may want to place your garage, family room, guest quarters, or other secondary rooms on a lower level, and use this lower level to support the upper main living level. This strategy was often utilized by Frank Lloyd Wright, as he favored elevating the main living floor as part of his design philosophy.

Your soils type will help dictate the extent to which you will be able to grade your site. If you encounter extreme rock conditions, or other soil barriers, you may want to use a column and floor joist design to keep costs down. I believe there is no need to try to put square pegs in round holes without good reason. The solid rock condition can be analyzed by an engineer for strength, and actually used to help in the design of your foundation. Also, the import of fill behind a well placed retainer or restrainer wall can dramatically reduce your need to deal with removing rock. I often see concrete slabs installed on difficult sites, when I must wonder if an alternate foundation style would have been more effective and less costly to install. Clearly I should not second guess a project I was not personally involved in, but I still have learned much over the years from watching the design and construction approach of others. I encourage you to explore this issue completely with your builder and designer/architect, if you have these conditions present on your building site.

THE TYPE OF SOIL, AND WHY IT MATTERS

The type of soils on your site is important due to both design and construction costs. **Your home needs the support of the soil for the weight of your home (bearing capacity), and you cannot take it for granted that the soil can support the load! Also, the soils type**

will impact the type of sewage system you need, if you are on a septic system.

There are three basic types of soil that we encounter, sand, clay and rock. Depending on which one, or more than one, you find on your site, your builder, and his team of professionals, will develop a plan designed to deal with the issues each type of soil presents. Is your soil good for compaction? Is it expansive and does it present the risk of damaging your foundation after completion? Does your design need special geotechnical engineering and design details to deal with solid rock conditions? Your builder and his/her professional team should provide satisfactory analysis of your soils conditions prior to design to be sure your design reflects the bearing capacity of your site (Grenier).

Most sub-divisions have a Soils Report, which is often a requirement of the sub-dividing process, and it provides an analysis of your soils type in selected areas of your neighborhood. This can provide an indication of what you might expect on your own building site. However, soils can be, and often are, very different in various areas of a typical sub-division. We have performed percolation tests, and soil profile excavations just fifty feet apart with remarkable differences in soil structure. In one case we experienced a four minute percolation rate (water absorption rate) in one area, while fifty feet away the percolation rate was 27 minutes. **In addition, there are geographic areas, such as the California coastline, where extreme danger of soil failure and collapse are a real issue, which means you will want to fully explore what type of soil is supporting your home!** The San Diego news has periodically covered stories of ocean front homes falling into the ocean, due to collapse of the soils supporting the home. In addition, the risk of losing a back yard due to excessive watering of the lawn exists in this type of soil (mainly when a steep slope is adjacent to the yard and home) (Grenier).

Your builder, designer/architect and structural engineer will use the bearing capacity analysis (by the geotechnical engineer) and other Soils Report information to determine the size and type of your foundation and many other issues. This is an important exercise. It should be noted that current code allows for estimation of the bearing capacity in some cases, or assuming a minimal bearing capacity per square foot of soil. This has historically ranged between 1000 and 1500 pounds per square foot, but each geographic area of the country is different, as the typical soils and engineering are often unique to the area. You may not need to be an engineer, but **be sure you ask questions concerning this issue, so you are fully informed as to the design of your home, whether buying or building!**

ABOUT MATERIALS MASONRY, FRAME, CONCRETE, STEEL, AND ALTERNATIVE MATERIALS

Typically the most economical choice for immediate cost of your project, and therefore higher equity, is to go with the flow and build the typical home for your region. This most often means building your home of frame with either a stucco exterior in most western states, or the typical siding in colder and wetter climates. In short, just like the existing projects you see all over town. However, there are other materials that provide improved longevity, aesthetic appeal, and energy efficiency, and often it is wise to use these materials when building your home. My experience has shown that in the large custom home market there are, for the most part, educated buyers that know the difference in quality products, and are willing to pay a little more for the quality and looks these materials add to the project.

I strongly recommend incorporating some of these items into your project, as long as the overall cost of the project does not get out of hand. Examples of choice we have made in the past are architectural details such as beam and plank ceilings, energy efficient windows, pre-cast concrete details on the exterior, steel exterior framing, quad-lock foam and concrete exterior walls, masonry exterior walls, special tile and granite counters and floors, T V and speaker surround sound wiring, computer and phone wiring and systems, quality custom cabinets, special interior hardwood doors, a great front door, and quality landscaping of the exterior. While your budget may not allow you to incorporate all of these items into your project, and it may not pencil out for the best equity position, some of these should be selectively included to add value and the "sizzle" that sells the project to a potential re-sale buyer. The old saying "There is never a second chance to make a first impression" is an essential wisdom to keep in mind while making your choices. Save where you can intelligently, but do not scrimp in areas that will cost you significant value in the end!

FLOOR PLAN, SIZE, AND BUDGET

Floor plan, size, and budget often are a product of where you need to locate your home on your building site. Also, **your floor plan is the basic foundation for all of the other working drawings required to build your home**, so you will want to be sure you are definite in your decision prior to going on to the exterior elevation phase of designing your home (Pitts).

Start by defining your ideal room size for each room in your home. For example, your ideal secondary bedroom size may be 12 feet x 14 feet while your master bedroom may need to be 15 feet x 22 feet in size. A quick analysis of your ideal room sizes, along with some simple math computations, will help you define the likely size of your home. Multiply each of the room sizes to arrive at the room square footage, add together all of the room square footage together, and then add 10% to 20% to allow for hallways and wall space. One of our typical four bedroom custom home designs will calculate to around 3200 to 3700 square feet, using this method. (see index)

An important concept to remember is that **you never have a second chance to make a first impression**. What this means for your floor plan is simply this. You should plan to place your living room and dining room near your entry area, as these are often the least used and best decorated areas of your home. In addition, you will want to take into consideration your views to the exterior of your home, and think about what a person entering your home will see from the time they approach your front door (Pitts). Visualize ringing your front door, passing through into your entry, and experiencing the environment to be created for your guest. **If you have beautiful building site views you will surely want to take full advantage of them while creating this experience!** If you do not have compelling views you can still create interest with interesting foyer features, glimpses into a well designed dining area, or featured views into a less used living area. Typically these two spaces are the least used, and allow for a good opportunity to create atmosphere for those entering your home for the first time. Be sure to focus on the details of this space when moving past the floor plan stage, and pay particular attention to the front door, floor coverings, ceiling height and treatments, wall details, lighting, and controlled view paths. (see step 3)

The topography of your home site will often require different approaches to foundations and subsequently necessitate flexibility with the traffic flow in your floor plan. This is where you meld your wants and needs as a home owner with your hopes to finish with a good investment too. The floor plan is a product of your lifestyle, which may mean different configurations to meet your needs. **Be sure to keep the floor plan relatively mainstream, as floor plans that are too unique often create re-sale problems.** Most buyers want similar type architecture and floor plans. Combining all of these issues can be difficult, but if done well it will help with your end appraisal and prospective equity (Barraza and Hansen).

HOA APPROVAL

Most Home Owner's Associations have an Architectural Control Committee that reviews and approves plans for the HOA. This can be in the form of a few home owners that meet periodically to review submitted plans, or in the form of a professional management company, which often includes the developer, and meets to review and approve proposed architectural improvements in the neighborhood. They often want to see any and all exterior improvement proposals from fencing to actual new homes. This is where your choice of a knowledgeable builder and architect/designer will pay off.

Most builders are willing to assume the responsibility of helping you with the HOA approval process. They are often faced with dealing with these committees and are likely able to deal with issues well that are likely to upset individual land owners when they are exposed to the sometimes annoying requests these committees issue. What color are you going to paint your home? What is the paint's Light Reflective Value (LRV)? What kind of material? How is the project oriented? Where do you plan to grade? How are you going to landscape when it is finished? Etc... etc... etc... All of these are legitimate questions for preserving the value of your neighborhood, but they are a source of stress for many homeowners, so you should let you builder and architect/designer handle these issues, if they are willing to take on the task.

STEP TWO DETAIL

Exterior elevations and design details, are related to how you want your home to look and feel for its curb appeal. Southwestern, Santa Fe, Mediterranean, Contemporary, Spanish Colonial, and many other choices you may like. Keep in mind two issues related to exterior curb appeal.

The first is that your neighborhood is likely to have an established architectural flavor, which it is in your best interest to follow. Why? Simply because your appraised value is often higher when the neighborhood is homogenous with regard to architectural design and feel (Barraza).

The second issue is cost of construction. Some styles are less costly to build due to the type and expense of the material and labor. Ask your builder about the costs to construct different styles you may like, and compare prior to deciding on your design. This issue is best explored early in the design process due to the extra expense in changing the design later.

EXTERIOR ELEVATIONS AND CURB APPEAL

At the risk of over use, I will re-state the old adage that **there is never a second chance to make a first impression**. Use the skills of your builder and designer/architect to fully explore the exterior design of your home, and equally important, how it will be situated on your building site. Try to visualize how it will look from your driveway and surrounding exposures. We have discussed this issue in detail in the design step part of this book, but I bring it up as a separate issue to emphasize the point that **you only have one chance at this, so use the experience and expertise of your professionals to do it right!** Ask questions, photograph completed projects you like, pull together your magazine tears, and you will improve the results of your own project.

STUCCO CHOICES AND ASSOCIATED ISSUES

Many homes now use a stucco exterior, and there are a number of good products on the market. We often see "Western One Coat", and many other brand names with various claims of superiority. I will not endorse or discuss the attributes of each of these here, as my main objective is you discuss the basic textures and the use of synthetic finishes.

Typically the Western One Coat type of stucco is applied as a base "brown" coat, which is allowed to dry and cure, and then later a texture coat is added. The basic texture choices are most often "lace", "river sand", or "silica sand". In addition, there is a synthetic choice, which includes your exterior color, and arrives pre-mixed from the factory in five-gallon buckets.

The Western One Coat base is applied in all of the above cases, and the texture coat is mixed on-site and applied over the top of the "brown" coat in every case except the synthetic option. The synthetic option involves the application of a pre-mixed material that will seal the exterior of your home with a water proof finish that has your home paint color mixed in, and is designed to reduce or eliminate most cracking situations. This is typically a more expensive option, though it sounds very appealing (reduced cracks and no painting!). However, synthetic stucco is not always a preferred choice! While it does seal your exterior and reduce or eliminate cracking, it also seals in moisture and **can cause significant future problems if moisture becomes present behind your wall or exterior finish!** Be sure to discuss this issue with your builder prior to choosing this option! (Nash)

Steven M. Washburn

The other choices offer a variety of different looks and features that you will want explore to be sure the appropriate finish is applied on your home. We often use lace on Mediterranean architecture, and one of the sand finishes on Southwestern styles. Also note that the sand finishes tend to show cracks more and are more expensive than the lace.

LARGE LOT ORIENTATION

A brief comment on large lot home placement is in order, due to the need to emphasize the need to think outside the box. We have had tremendous success with projects that do not fit the traditional square orientation to the road and driveway. I encourage full exploration of the building site, views, sun exposure and topography to arrive at the best orientation and placement of your home on the building site. We often successfully place our homes in these non-traditional orientations with exceptional results. (See discussion in step 1)

STEP THREE DETAIL

Interior elevations, ceiling heights, and interior details are next in line for design decisions. We suggest the ceiling heights in the larger living area to be approximately 11 to 14 feet, as it is most often appropriate for the size of these rooms. Bedroom and smaller room ceilings are most often best at from 8 to 10 feet in height. In addition, your kitchen will feel more intimate and cozy with 8 to 10 foot ceilings as well.

Interior elevations may also include some wood beams, vigas, niches, arches, shelves, fireplaces, and numerous other architectural details that add to the interior atmosphere of your home. (see the various ceiling heights shown in the photos below)

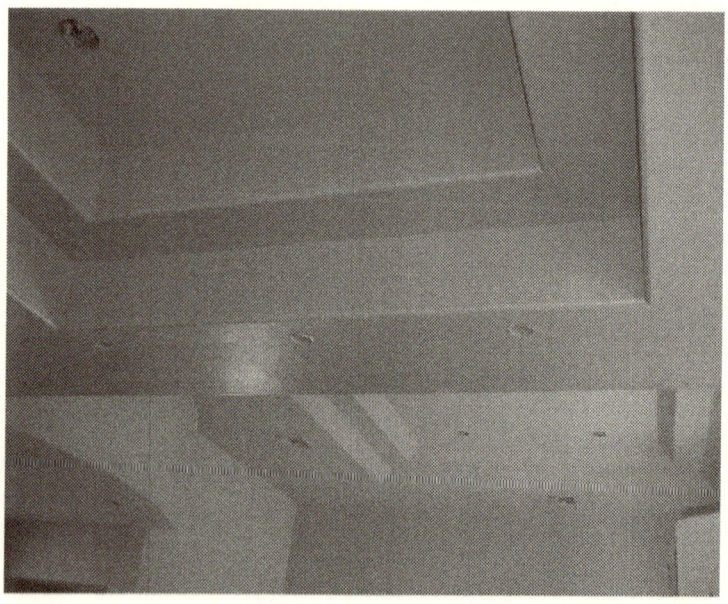

Interior Design by Design Solutions

Note the use of a lower tray type ceiling in the kitchen area combined with a higher coffered ceiling in the nearby family room. The hallway is to the left, which includes a radius dropped ceiling at the entrance to the family room.

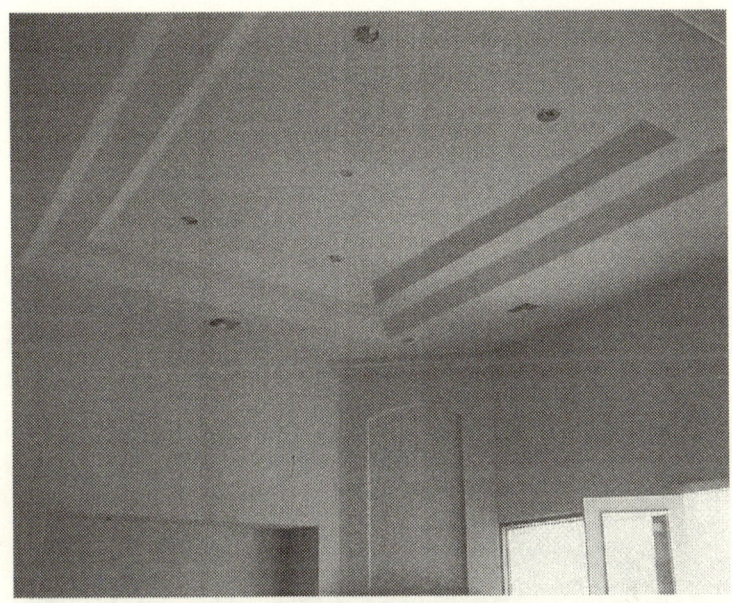

Interior Design by Design Solutions

Here is another look at this same ceiling from another direction.

Interior Design by Design Solutions

Here is one more photo looking from the family room into the hallway and kitchen area. Note the use of ceiling detail to enhance the design. (Pitts)

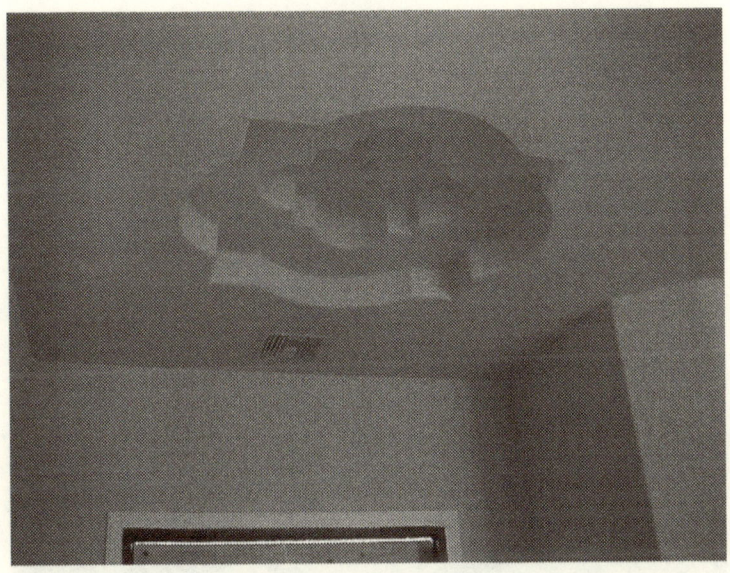

Interior Design by Design Solutions, framing by GES Company

Here is a very unusual ceiling detail, that was designed to mirror the detail of the pre-cast concrete windows near the entry and bathrooms of this home.

Design by Ollanik Company, framing by GES Company

Note the back patio in this picture does not have a step down (floors are the same level as the main house), and the use of picture framed arches enhances rather than taking away from the city views below. (The bottom of this photo is where the exterior doors will be placed)

Architectural Design by Design Solutions, finish by Stronghold Drywall

Here is an example of a very open dining room floor plan. Two open archways announce the entry into the room, while the hanging light fixture adds to the atmosphere of the room. Also, the hallway is drawn into the room by adding cabinets and niches.

PATIO CHOICES (ROOF, CEILING AND FLOORS)

Patios are currently being thought of as an extension of the interior living space. To make this desire more of a reality we are altering the design in a number of ways. The first is to keep the floor elevation at (or near) the same level as the interior floor level, so long as water issues are not present (a roof over the patio and no drainage problems). In addition, the floor finish can be the same as the interior, and door closets can be used to allow for a completely open transition between interior and patio traffic flow. Fireplaces are often added, as are Bar-B-Q grills and even full exterior kitchens in some cases. Also, adding an interesting type ceiling (beams, and tongue and groove) can help make this area feel more like interior.

You may or may not want this type of lifestyle for yourself, but be sure to think ahead for re-sale, as planning for these features during your initial construction is much less expensive than remodeling later.

STEP FOUR DETAIL

Window and exterior door choices help create environment from both an interior and exterior stand point, though you will want to choose within your budget. We most often use a liberal amount of large picture windows, that do not open, but provide unobstructed views while also helping to reduce the window budget. For example, in a typical bay window, or breakfast room, configuration we often install a large picture window as the center window with two single hung side windows that provide cross ventilation. This accomplishes the tasks of creating an appealing room feel, providing unobstructed views, and keeping prices low! There are also placement and engineering issues that are too numerous to discuss in this brief format. You will find more detailed information in our design publication.

Door choices will likely be based on your personal taste, though I suggest selections based on value and durability. For many of our clients this often means choosing between insulated metal French single-lite doors or the more prestigious Pella aluminum clad wood door systems. Yes, we like the Pella best, but the metal doors also provide an appealing painted door that is also affordable. We tend to discourage the installation of plain wood doors due to UV deterioration and potential maintenance problems which often occur with these doors.

Be sure to plan for these in the design phase, as your exterior engineering requires lateral stability analysis, which is costly to change if your window and door openings change later.

WINDOW CHOICES AND COSTS

Window placement both within the room and where they occur horizontally and vertically is critical to several issues. The size and shape of your window will impact the cost of the window, the lateral engineering required to reinforce the wall penetration required for your window, and the impact of your exterior elevation and views. Our typical choices are as follows, though your builder and designer/architect may have other ideas and justifications for your geographic area. Listen to their reasoning, but make an informed decision that works for you!

1)   The top of your window, "header", should typically be not less than eight feet from your finished floor in a custom home. Higher headers are often used in areas where the views or ceiling heights allow, but rarely do we go below eight feet. (tract housing typically has used seven feet in many regions of the U.S.)

2)   Try to avoid placing window frame breaks for multiple window units in a place where the view is obstructed. For example: When installing a 6 foot tall picture window along with a 2 foot tall operational window, be sure to place the picture window on top, and plan the window sill low enough to allow for an unobstructed view. This sounds like a simple enough process, but it is often overlooked and lamented over for years after the mistake is made!

3) Be sure of the size, shape and placement of your windows prior to releasing the plans to the engineer. Why? Because the window opening will likely require a lateral engineering analysis, which may need to be re-calculated if a window is later changed. The lateral analysis involves calculating the effects of wind and other natural stresses on a building, and your window opening leaves a weak void that must be compensated for with other structural components.

Buy the best windows your budget allows! Windows have a "U" value that measures energy efficiency, and usually are made of aluminum, vinyl, or wood. We like Milguard aluminum, Window Mart vinyl, and Pella wood windows, as we have had excellent experience with each of these products from both a service and product standpoint. From a budgeting standpoint, the aluminum are the least expensive, while the vinyl are usually about 30%-50% more, and the wood are typically approximately 3-times the cost of aluminum, though many of my clients prefer these for both the quality look and feel, and better insulation factors.

We have installed all of the window packages mentioned above, and find that owner's can help meet tight budgets with the aluminum products, but always prefer the Pella type wood windows, and they have never expressed regret at choosing the best quality.

Another important issue is the planning of window sills for your window coverings etc... You may want deep set windows, or windows that are set in from the exterior wall a few inches to allow for less water drainage over your glass and a more custom look. This can impact both your exterior trim work (pre-cast concrete trim etc...) and will certainly reduce the width of your window sill. Remain aware of this issue while deciding on windows and trim, as they all go together, and will likely be overlooked, as most designers/architects and builders will not discuss this subject as a priority. It will often be up to the owner to communicate how strongly you feel about this issue. Also, if you choose wide interior window sills, you may want to add tile on the sills to reduce maintenance and improve interior design.

COLORS AND TEXTURES

Colors, textures, product selections, and special features can be chosen after the design process. However, you may want to incorporate these into your plan along with locations of speakers, audio-visual, and computers. Deciding on these issues during design is possible if you can visualize well. Our clients often use the services of an interior designer to accomplish this task, and there are also coordinators available through some tile and painting sub-contractors and suppliers. Ask your builder for a shopping list for your allowance items, and which suppliers providing design services as part of their package.

A DISCUSSION ON HVAC AND ENERGY EFFICIENCY

A high efficiency heating and air conditioning system is a smart investment! I recently built two 3200 to 3300 square foot (heated and cooled space) homes that were the same plan, same North Eastern view orientation, same insulation, same windows, and same sub-contractors. In short, it was nearly an identical house, with one exception. One owner asked for a high efficiency 13 SEER TRANE Air conditioner, while the other settled for a 10 SEER unit from another manufacturer. July came and went, and I asked each of the owners what their electric bill was for July. The answers surprised me! The 10 SEER home's electric bill was over $500 while the 13

SEER TRANE home came in at less than $300 for the same period. The only variable I could not verify was the actual temperature setting of each thermostat. However, the difference was still amazing to say the least.

To obtain the best energy efficiency there are many relatively economical choices. Among the easiest are insisting on an energy rated house for your area! In our region this requires actual duct leakage testing performed by either the electric or gas company, which shows the actual air leakage of your duct work. Along with this test, be sure your return air plenum is hard duct, and not simply a sealed drywall and frame cavity below your furnace! Industry experts tell us that 50% of duct leakage occurs at this point, so a hard duct plenum is no longer an option, it is a must. (TEP) Also each Air Conditioner unit has a SEER, Standard Energy Efficiency Rating, which measures its use of electricity. The higher the number the more efficient the unit. Low efficiency units are currently rated at 10 SEER, while 11, 12 and some 13 (effective) SEER ratings are now available. TRANE even offers one they bill as an effective 16 SEER, which blends a 5-ton compressor with a built in 2.5 ton compressor that replaces the efforts, and power usage, of the 5 ton compressor when the work load permits. (Hamstra) This combined with a variable speed fan, that communicates with the compressor, allows for an effective increase in the SEER rating estimates. Yes, it is more expensive, but we have successfully installed this type unit in large custom homes with more than one zone, with excellent results. This is an excellent choice, though more expensive to install initially.

Debates still rage on as to whether Heat Pumps or Gas heating are best, and for sure the electric companies and gas companies both have excellent arguments for their sources of heat and A/C. However, there is no debate as to the better SEER rated units making total sense in a new project! We most often install 12 and effective 13 SEER ratings, with some of the top rated TRANE equipment chosen by clients as well. Also, I have yet to hear a client complain about a too efficient system or an electric bill that was too low!

INTERIOR DOOR CHOICES

Your interior door budget can range between roughly $85 to $575 per door, depending upon your choices. The $85 door is either a six or four panel hollow core masonite pre-hung door that is painted, and often used in spec homes to provide a quality look at a low price. This is often the best choice, if you are trying to stay on budget, and do not want stained doors.

Stain grade fir, hemlock, or pine doors are usually the next step up, at a cost range of $225 to $275 per pre-hung door, and these are my choice whenever possible. We like these due to the overall quality look when they are finished with a nice stain, and they are not usually a budget buster.

The most expensive doors we typically install are hardwood knotty alder doors, and have ranged in price from $475 to $575 per pre-hung door. These are absolutely beautiful and worth the money if you are either building in an area that can support the extra expense from an appraisal stand point, or you plan to live in your home for a long period and enjoy the atmosphere these doors help create in your home.

Trim work around your doors or rounded corners, along with base board choices are issue related to your door jamb selections. Whether you choose tiled base board, wood base board, or no base board at all, you will want to also decide if you like rounded corners that will be finished with sheet rock and metal and then painted, or the use of finish carpentry. The finish carpentry will usually involve more costs, as the trim work and installation most often is more costly than drywall. However, your choice to add detail will affect the atmosphere you are creating in your interior design, and nicely stained wood trim will often add to the look and feel of quality interior design. I often choose the rounded corners for Southwestern and Santa Fe styles, and lean towards wood trim in Mediterranean and more formal architectural styles. This is only my preference, and you should determine the best style for your own tastes. This is a good time to go through your magazine tears to review the photos you selected for initial design influence.

Review the photos below to help determine the impact you gravitate towards.

Custom alder front doors by Fairfield Custom Woodwork

Here is a custom built front door system that is installed with rounded corners and no wood trim. Arched tops often require specially milled trim, so this owner elected to remove the extra expense, as she liked the simple look. Also note there is no base trim at the floor. Some owners choose no base while others prefer either wood or tile base. In addition, the eight foot door height enhances the first impression (many exterior doors are seven feet high).

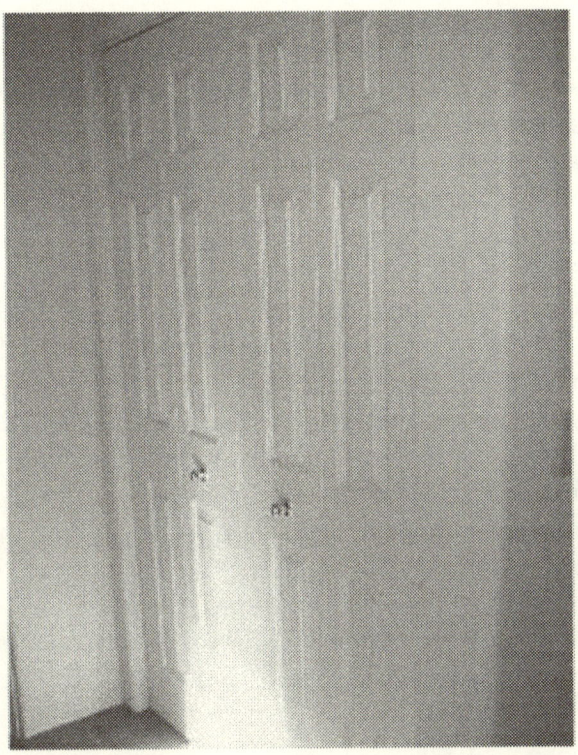

Here is a look at a raised panel paint grade door, that is much less expensive than stain grade wood doors. Also note there is not trim on this door as well. (rounded drywall corners)

PLUMBING FIXTURE CHOICES

Plumbing fixtures come in a variety of design and quality. There are expensive cast fixtures in finishes ranging from stainless to hand rubbed nickel and even gold plated. You will likely want to hit a budget for your project, so I suggest prioritizing your fixtures with the higher quality fixtures in the more visible areas of your home, and the lower end fixtures in areas such as your laundry room, where they will most likely be less important. A $69.00 single leaver Moen faucet may be perfectly O K in your laundry, while you would probably want to use a much nicer Grohe (or higher end brand) in your kitchen and primary bathrooms. You should still be able to remain on a budget, if this is an issue, by mixing these qualities, and still achieve the look and feel of a truly custom home.

The plumbing fixture budget can get out of hand in a hurry, especially when you visit a showroom with all of the fancy new gizmos created to make your home a show place of plumbing inventions. Ask your builder for a previous package that he/she has installed that is within your budget, and take this with you when you go shopping! With this information you are more likely to remain on track with regard to your budget. Also, keep in mind that most states are experiencing water shortage issues, so try to select low water use fixtures in order to help conserve our resources. (see discussion on water issues to determine the need for water softener, reverse osmosis system, or water pathogen treatment options that may be needed)

LOW VOLTAGE WIRING

Low voltage wiring is simply your TV, telephone, audio, alarm, intercom and some yard lighting, and can range from very low cost to thousands of dollars, depending upon your selections. At the very least you will want to spend a few dollars on surround sound speaker wiring in the main entertainment areas of your home, usually the family and master bedrooms. You may also choose to hire an audio visual specialist and/or a computer network specialist to install specialized system wiring to meet your needs. This wiring typically is installed just prior to sealing your walls with sheetrock or plaster, so start shopping early to allow sufficient time for selection and installation.

LIGHTING FIXTURE CHOICES

Here is where you will certainly want to spend some time thinking through the atmosphere and interior decorating you are trying to create in your new home. Lighting in commercial and residential interior design will impact how you feel when spending time in the finished product. Think about how you feel in commercial buildings with high acoustical tile ceilings that are loaded with rows of long florescent lights. Then think about your favorite restaurant, and how the lighting there is used to create an intimate atmosphere, and therefore a more romantic setting for meals and conversation. Your choices of ceiling heights, textures, and lighting types will have a similar impact on your own home's environment.

Architectural Design by Design Solutions

This entry utilizes hanging fixtures that may not be appropriate for a lower entry area on some homes. Wall mounted fixtures can also provide interesting light patterns reflected on your walls, and are most often used by designers. Also note the use of foam and stucco details on this home, along with a wrought iron gate and pre-cast concrete column caps to add additional detail and texture.

Stucco system by Koedecker and Kenyon company

Here is a close-up of Spanish Lace stucco on the wall, sand finish on the ceiling, and the use of exterior ceiling fans to enhance the North East exposed back patio area. Also note the use of vinyl windows (mid price range)

Here is an example of lamps controlled by a wall switch, recessed can lights (on a dimmer switch), and a Casa Blanca fan to help create atmosphere in the bedroom. Also note the seven foot window headers.

Lighting fixture choices are very similar to the plumbing fixture choice strategy discussed above. There can be a mixture of high end and moderately priced fixtures used to achieve a custom look without blowing the budget. Careful selection in the main living area is how we approach this task, with the largest part of the budget used in dining room chandeliers, breakfast rooms, bathrooms and entry areas. Laundry rooms, closets, garages and secondary areas usually are assigned florescent lighting or other less expensive lights. Some other rooms may be important to you, and you will want to prioritize these issues for yourself.

A quick reminder that the number of recessed can lighting you choose can impact your home's energy efficiency. The hole through your ceiling required to install these lights can allow air to move between the living area and the attic space, which can reduce energy efficiency significantly. In some geographic regions (usually dryer climates) you can install the attic insulation tight up to the roof deck, which can help with this issue (TEP). However, I suggest the reduction of recessed can lighting to those lights that you feel are necessary to achieve your living needs. Remember to use lamps and half hot electrical receptacles (places where you can plug in your lamp and turn it on from a wall switch) to enhance your lighting atmosphere.

Typically the electrician will install your recessed can lighting, and you need only select the trim color, most often black or white. Other lighting selections are usually wall sconces, hanging fixtures, under cabinet lighting, fluorescents, low-voltage yard lighting, exterior spotlights, and special use task lighting. Ask your builder where he/she purchases these items at wholesale, and schedule an afternoon to spend with the salesperson, armed with your budget allowance and the electrical plan page of your blue prints, of course. This can be a fun afternoon, especially if it is with someone like our dear Melba, who knows how to help clients make good lighting environment decisions.

CUSTOM CABINETS (OR) PRODUCTION LINE MANUFACTURED CABINETS

Most homeowners do not think about the cabinets in their home. However, this woodwork can help add to the quality look of your home, or it can take away, if the woodwork is sub-standard and viewed as a "cheap" product. We like the custom cabinets we install because they enhance the atmosphere of the home, are functional and durable, and you are not left with the feeling that you are compromising your choice of quality for cost reduction that you will want to change at a later date. It is very difficult and expensive to change cabinets after a home is complete, so spend a little more on this product now, and save on something else that is much less trouble to replace later. Ask your builder to meet with the cabinet maker, so you can review kitchen traffic flow, appliance locations, and style of cabinetry to be installed. Also, ask for stain samples, and be sure to write down the stain for communication with the painter for your beams, doors, windows and other stained items. You will likely want them to match!

Custom alder cabinetry by Fairfield, Granite by Granite Creations

This kitchen uses under counter lighting, hanging and recessed can lights to provide light and atmosphere. It also utilizes custom alder cabinets, granite counter tops mixed with lighter tile to brighten the space and add extra texture. The cabinets are the foundation of this room, and provide one of the most important components to a quality and stylish look. Counters and lighting details are relatively easy to change later, but cabinet changes are much more difficult and expensive. We suggest starting with an excellent cabinet, then adding the best you can afford for the other details.

Steven M. Washburn

COUNTER TOP CHOICES

Counter tops range from low cost laminates to tile, granite and other specialized surfaces. I most often recommend either granite or a well designed tile installation for custom home bath and kitchens. The granite look is a little more expensive, but it helps provide the atmosphere that buyers and realtors say is most desirable. Tile is typically less expensive and is still a good choice, if you need to reduce expense to meet your budget. Laminates are always a last resort to meet a budget, and can be replaced at a later date without too much trouble in removing them to make room for tile or granite.

A special note with granite for chefs! Keep it sealed or use another surface! Food preparation can allow organic penetration into the granite, which could allow bacteria to grow, which is clearly not a healthy situation! Take steps to prevent this problem, or choose another surface! Corian?

Flooring by Handcrafted Tile Co, Cabinets by Fairfield and Granite Creations

Another kitchen example with knotty alder cabinets, granite counters, a central skylight, and paneled refrigerator. Also note the use of the large floor tile (travertine), and recessed lighting.

FLOOR TILE AND CARPET, THE SMART CHOICES

Volumes can be, and I sure have been, written on this subject, so I will not explore the details of tile and carpet here. I simply want to explore the smartest choices from a budget standpoint. We typically install tile and carpet in areas of the home that make the most sense. This improves the appeal and livability, including maintenance, while keeping an eye on cost.

One of our typical custom homes will have ceramic tile installed in the foyer, halls, baths, kitchen, laundry and any other high traffic area. The rest of the home is typically carpeted for both comfort and affordability, as carpet tends to be less expensive. Your choices here will have a significant impact on the budget of your home, and you may very well decide to install much more tile than recommended. However, keep in mind the impact to the overall budget, and realize that extra money spent here will not always show up on an appraisal.

SHOWER AND TUB FINISHES, A DISCUSSION OF POSSIBILITIES

Fiberglass units? Cultured marble? Custom tile? Granite? Marble? Special glass block and glass door enclosures? I always want to spend a lot on kitchens and bathrooms, as these are my favorite areas to express a little creativity. However, spending money here can get out of hand, so I recommend setting a budget and sticking to it, if you want to keep your equity position as high as possible. I recommend large (At least 16 inch X 16 inch) ceramic tile **installed in a diamond shaped pattern** for both shower and tub walls, and either smaller or mosaic tumbled tile for the shower floors. A little extra should also be spent on a simple, but appealing, border pattern to help make the area look more custom. Meet with the installer and your builder to discuss the possibilities and skills of your particular installer. Remember that your installer works in this field every day, so they likely have some interesting ideas that they have already installed in other projects.

Why am I not suggesting any of the other materials listed above? Because from a cost vs. quality standpoint I have had the best experience with the formula listed above. It works and buyers like it!

The use of a hand painted bowl and six inch Saltillo tile provides a southwestern flavor for this guest home vanity.

Tile by Handcrafted Tile Company

This tub deck (tile over a framed base) provides an interesting and relatively low cost frame for this master bedroom Jacuzzi tub. Also note the selection of tiled vanities and porcelain sinks. The tub faucet is a Jacuzzi water fall (at right near window) that is relatively low priced compared to many other fixtures, and is often preferred, as it blends with the tub finish. (see control valves at the left side near the vanity)

PAINTING OPTIONS

Why do we need to discuss paint? The painter sprays it on and that's it. right? Well not exactly. These days we face HOA approval in some neighborhoods that restrict colors and light reflective values. Also, interior and exterior colors and choices should coordinate with your stain, tile and other interior color and texture selections, so that your interior look all ties together as an appealing environment. This may include some special faux painted walls, which are often used by interior decorators today. Also, you will want to choose from flat, egg shell, low sheen, or semi-gloss interior paint sheens. In addition, there are exterior paint choices. A "hot spot" primer is designed to help reduce or eliminate the calcium bleed through that can occur in new stucco walls. You will also want to choose the type and quality of your exterior paint, and whether you should include a sealer, because many exterior paints do allow water penetration. Take some time to discuss these issues with your builder to be sure your paint reflects your wants and needs. It is much more expensive to paint your home after it is furnished and landscaped!

LANDSCAPE, HARDSCAPE, AND OTHER CHOICES THAT WILL MAKE YOUR PROJECT LOOK FINISHED

Just as your interior door, window, cabinet, flooring, countertop and paint choices create an interior atmosphere, your hardscape and landscaping will help create exterior atmosphere and curb appeal. I only mention this issue to call it to your attention in hopes that you will include it into your budget in a significant way. Most Home Owner's Associations now require landscape plans to improve the value and appearance of their neighborhood. I recently read in the Phoenix Arizona newspaper that the city was increasing their enforcement of exterior cleanliness and landscape for all neighborhoods. A modest design and installation of a few key walk ways, landscape walls, and plantings will be all that is needed in most cases, and can be achieved either on your own, or by a professional arranged by your contractor. The end result will help your appraised value too!

Flagstone patio by Handcrafted Tile Company

This backyard is hardscape with real flagstone and landscaped with colored gravel and low water use plantings. Other less expensive choices could have been all colored gravel, colored concrete, bomenite (looks like flagstone, but has a concrete base), or brick pavers.

A BRIEF DISCUSSION ON WATER QUALITY ISSUES

WATER QUALITY ISSUES

Water quality and availability is becoming a front burner issue in more and more communities, so a brief discussion on this issue is appropriate in the context of your building choices. Basic potable, municipal, water quality is regulated by the Environmental Protection Agency, EPA, and consists of primary and secondary regulations designed to keep drinking water safe for human consumption. The EPA regulates streams and rivers, sewage treatment effluent discharge into the environment, and primary and secondary drinking water standards. (Nathanson 2000)

The **primary standards** are for the most part designed to make the water free of live pathogens (disease free) safe to drink, and there are three basic ways this is accomplished. Most municipal water companies are likely to do the following to assure compliance with these regulations. Filtering to remove sediment, and then treating the water with one or more of the following: Chlorine to kill pathogens and leave a residual in the water to continue killing new pathogens, after the organic materials are removed to acceptable levels: Ozone, where it is installed, which also kills pathogens, but does not leave a residual in the water to continue killing any new pathogens: Ultra-violet light treatment, which is now often the treatment of choice to kill pathogens, but also does not leave a residue in the water to continue killing future pathogens that may be present. (Nathanson, 2000)

The **secondary standards** are for the most part concerned with the long term issues of water quality, or what does not kill or make you sick right away. These are generally heavy metals, dissolved insecticides and toxic substances that are often found in water supplies. There is a specific list of these substances as well as specific ppm, parts per million, measurements that municipal water companies are required to meet prior to distribution. Some of these are Lead, Mercury, Copper, Fluoride, Arsenic and a long list of other undesirable substances. Some of these, including Fluoride, are desirable, but only at certain levels that do not harm the health of the population. (Clark)

Neither the primary or secondary standards are concerned with the hardness of the water, the amounts of dissolved solids such as calcium and magnesium that reduce the effectiveness of your detergents, and can damage your clothing over the long run. These are best dealt with by water treatment systems that you will want to discuss with your contractor. In addition, the EPA standards for drinking water quality do not always assure you truly safe water, so you may also want to install a reverse osmosis system under your kitchen sink, and at other key locations in your home, to be as safe as possible with regard to your drinking water. These reverse osmosis units currently cost around $600 installed, and are generally available. Also, in cases where you have a well, or you feel the need to treat for pathogens in addition to the municipal treatment, you may want to install an UV unit on your home water supply, which are now available at reasonable prices for home use.

If you are planning to use a private water well, you will also want to know about nitrates. Nitrate emissions are part of the secondary EPA standards for municipal water systems, and are a health public issue, especially for very young children. Nitrates occur in nature, and are added to the environment from livestock manure, human sewage, and agricultural fertilizer. Nitrates not processed as plant nutrients travel very slowly from the earth's surface into the water table as the water percolates through porous soil. Sources of nitrate pollution into private water wells are often due to septic systems and agriculture fertilization (Clark). In addition, shallow wells are much more at risk than deeper wells. For example: If your well is between 100 and 200 feet deep, and you have a septic system or agriculture nearby, you run a significant risk of nitrates entering your water system. To improve your nitrate pollution risks you will want take several steps:

1) Install your septic system as far away from your well as possible, and try to place it down hill from the well! (at least 100 feet is typical code) Also, maintain your septic system according to your contractor's suggested schedule.

2) If you are installing a new well, drill as deep as your well contractor says he/she can. Water, and therefore nitrates, move very slowly through soils, so deeper is better, as the water will be drawn from deeper in the water aquifer.

3) Test your water at least annually! You will want to enlist the services of your local water treatment professional to keep track of your water quality on a regular basis.

4) Connect to the sewer system, if and when you have municipal sewer available.

STEP FIVE DETAIL

Your Check Set is simply a finished (or nearly finished) set of working drawings that typically involves from ten to twenty pages of blue prints (more in larger more detailed homes). These are the instructions to all of the trades that will allow them to work together as symphony rather than as a group of disjointed individuals that build in the vacuum of their individual responsibilities. Your involvement in reviewing the Check Set is mainly related to assuring you have all of the important items you requested included in your finished set of plans.

The pages you will want to review should be familiar to you by now due to your active participation in the design process. These are most often the floor plan, exterior elevations, lighting and electrical plan, landscape and yard plan, and interior elevations. Other detail pages are HVAC, plumbing, grading, site plan, roofing plan, framing plan, engineering pages, and other sheets you will most likely be less interested in reviewing. These additional pages should reflect the decisions you made during the initial design phase. For example: You may have determined that you wanted the best in energy efficiency, and approved return air ducts in each bedroom, a high efficiency TRANE A/C unit, and a combination of hard and flexible duct work. Plumbing issues may include installation of a recirculation pump for hot water, a soft water loop, and the type of plumbing pipes you prefer.

These should already be on your blue prints, and you will want to simply ask your builder or designer to be sure. Last minute changes are typically much less expensive prior to beginning construction, so this exercise is important to your overall budget and ease of construction.

STEP SIX DETAIL

BUILDING PERMITS

The history of building permits is very interesting and range from the early years of "just tell me where you are building and pay your fee" to today when the issuing county or municipality wants to know many details of your project, and they also now have very specific rules governing those very same items.

A typical building permit can involve these basic issues. Zoning, Addressing, Grading and Hillside Development, Wastewater and Department of Environmental Quality, Native Plant and Species Preservation, Electrical, Mechanical, Plumbing, Heating and Air Conditioning, Structural Design, Engineering Calculations, Handicapped Standards, and more issues being added annually.

You will certainly want your builder and architect/designer to handle the permitting process, as this has certainly become a very specialized industry. There are now companies springing up that deal only with processing building and development plans not just for large developments, but now for individual home permits as well. I regularly see these professional plan processors at our four local permitting municipalities, and they are always busy. I suggest using your builder for this process, as it will help keep costs down and speed along the process for your construction schedule.

WHAT YOU WILL NEED FOR YOUR MORTGAGE APPLICATION

Typically your mortgage company will want four items from you and your builder, aside from the typical income documentation and mortgage application. These are a complete **set of plans** for an appraisal, **your specification information** showing the materials and products that you plan to use in the construction of your home, an **itemized cost breakdown, or budget**, showing the total cost of your project, and a **copy of your contract** with your builder. (Cummings)

A short discussion about your builder is in order concerning this part of your project. It has been my experience that your mortgage lender wants to be sure that your builder is financially stable, and can complete your project according to the plans and specifications they are using to establish value for your loan. The appraiser uses the plans and specifications, along with the cost breakdown and comparable sales in your neighborhood, to develop an appraisal for a property that does not yet exist. Therefore, your choice of builder may not always be the least expensive choice, but often he/she may submit a budget that is a little higher than other builders estimate. It is very important to remember that a realistic budget is important. Look for a builder that will shoot straight with you rather than one who just tells you what you want to hear! A realistic budget allows you the opportunity to make choices early in the project, so that you can affect the end cost of your project.

There is price and there is cost, and often times the lowest price does not always result in the lowest overall cost. **In the past year alone, I have been referred two large custom homes where the builders had difficulty in this area, and we took over the jobs to help the clients meet their budgeting requirements to finish their projects. It is interesting to note that in both cases the lender was key to the referral.**

CHAPTER 3

MISCELLANEOUS ISSUES OF CONCERN

TERMITE PROTECTION

Termites? Why should you be concerned with insects? Our termite treatment issues are best told through a story repeated by Dave, owner of Security Pest Control, of a beautiful new home (constructed by another builder), built on a solid rock hill. It was painstakingly constructed with only the best materials and looked absolutely wonderful when it was finally complete. Less than two years after completion the owner discovered termites, Dave tells how the owner secured bids for re-treatment and an on-going guarantee for his home. The lowest bid was in the thousands of dollars, as was the on-going guarantee associated with this project. In addition, I have seen numerous projects that required re-treatment involving drilling of slabs and the associated time and money spent by individuals choosing the traditional termite treatment method. I suggest combining the traditional method with an underground plumbing re-treatment system for concrete slab foundations. This would have been an inexpensive solution for the projects mentioned above.

We have used this type system for over ten-years, and it allows for easy re-treatment, without unsightly drilling and plugging.

Since the E.P.A. outlawed the use of most of the older and more effective chemicals, termites have been, and will likely continue to be a problem. In my experience, an excellent pro-active termite plan is essential to preserve long term value for your project. I have heard many people say that if they build out of steel, masonry or concrete, then they have little worry about termites. This is just not true! Termites will eat many other items in your home other than the exterior structure, so be sure your builder has a sound plan to deal with this issue over the long haul, not just for the warranty period! I use an underground plumbing system in most of our projects that allows for re-treating with chemicals under the concrete after the project is complete. (O'Shaunesy) My theory is that if a new chemical is discovered that is more effective, then we will be able to re-introduce the chemical under the slab without drilling, as is currently the practice for re-treating. Also, re-treating is simple and low cost with this system, and it does not add significantly to the cost of the project. In fact, one treatment of a similar home that required drilling was 20% more expensive than the installation of our plumbing system, plus the drilling made a mess and the home owner had to stay home all day to deal with the mess. Planning for re-treatment is essential to successfully dealing with termites today!

ENERGY EFFICIENCY AND ASSOCIATED ISSUES

ENERGY EFFICIENCY

Your builder and designer/architect will be able to help you build energy efficiency into your design and construction in a number of basic ways. Here are the very basic issues you will want to know, that in the end will make a significant impact on your home's energy use and livability.

1) Where possible, for the least exposure to the hot summer sun, orient your home in such a way that the window exposure to the South and West sides of your home are either minimal or covered by porches.

2) Be sure you select at least R-30 ceiling and R-19 wall insulation, and up-grade to higher "R" values if possible in your budget.

3) Make sure your framer installs a foam strip below the bottom plate of each exterior wall, to seal for air leakage, and to provide additional insect protection.

4) Buy the best windows your budget allows! Windows have a "U" value that measures energy efficiency, and usually are made of aluminum, vinyl, or wood. We like Milguard aluminum, Window Mart vinyl, and Pella wood windows, as we have had excellent experience with each of these products from both a service and product standpoint. From a budgeting standpoint, the aluminum are the least expensive, while the vinyl are usually about 30%-50% more, and the wood are typically approximately 3-times the cost of aluminum.

5) Be sure your builder builds your home to the current energy efficiency standards for your area, which will involve all of the above, and several other components that may be unique to your geographic region.

Southwest Gas and T E P have specific energy efficiency programs called Energy Advantage Plus and T E P Guarantee home program. Also, there is the Sun Share program designed to add photovoltaic generators to your home, which are sponsored by the T E P electric utility, and have the potential of growing in popularity around the country. However, these are the current basics for energy efficient building.

Exterior walls, framing details, insulation, energy efficient windows and doors, testing your duct work for leakage, selecting an efficient (high SEER rated air conditioner or heat pump), and sealing under your walls and at every opening of your home is critical to assuring an energy efficient home. (SW Gas) The gas and electric utilities in most communities have inspection programs that are designed to assure that your home is built with energy efficiency in mind. All of the above issues are important, and there are other issues that will be specific to your area of the country, so be sure to ask you builder what he/she builds into your project to make it energy efficient.

A BRIEF DISCUSSION ON CODE COMPLIANCE

In 2001 and 2002 many government entities began to switch from the UBC, Uniform Building Code, to the IRC, International Residential Code. The switch was supposed to be an improvement, but has caused significant problems, especially related to masonry construction. I do not plan to fully explore the issues of these changes here in this publication. However, I call it to your attention so you will be aware that there are very significant changes to working drawing, engineering, and construction practices that will likely impact your project. **Ask your builder and architect/designer if they are familiar with the change, and be sure you select professionals that can help you through the detailed requirements of this change.**

YOUR HOA AND OTHER MISCELLANEOUS ISSUES

HOME OWNER'S ASSOCIATION, ARCHITECTURAL COMMITTEE, DUES, RULES, AND CC&R RESTRICTIONS.

I often hear complaints about Home Owner's Associations, and you will want to know if there is one, along with any associated CC&R restrictions. However, keep in mind that these associations help preserve and build value to your project. (Diamond) Your area would be less valuable if the neighbors had a '56 Chevy on blocks and a construction yard located in plain view! All of that being said, it is helpful to enlist the services of your designer and builder in dealing with these associations, especially if they are familiar with the rules and personalities of an individual association. It has been my experience that obtaining the HOA approval is often just as difficult and time consuming as processing the entire set of plans for building permits. Your builder should be willing to help you in this process as part of his/her overall responsibilities. He/she will help assure you can build the style and size home you want during the design review process. Also, you will want to be sure you read the CC&R rules, and understand your rights, responsibilities, and costs associated with the development. Who knows, you may want to serve in one of the HOA positions!

A DISCUSSION ON IMPACT FEES AND TAXES

I feel compelled to include a short discussion on "soft costs" which are being added at an ever increasing rate to new construction. In many communities, ours included, there are new fees, and increasing old fees, being added to the cost of a new home. These fees are not readily evident to the home buyer, though they are a definite expense and add thousands of dollars to a project. While I do agree that new construction should pay its way in infrastructure costs, there must be a balance to these expenses to avoid choking off the economic activity and jobs created by your choice to buy or build your dream home. In short, if you cannot afford to build there will be no associated economic activity or related jobs. I encourage you to take part in your local discussion on these issues and make your voice known to the decision makers in your community. We all need to be responsible citizens, but some of these fees are cumbersome and counterproductive to the community at large.

Here is an example of the fees added to one of our recent projects:

Total project cost approximately $480,000.

RELATED APPROXIMATE EXTRA COSTS

Prime contractor tax $29,000.
Sewer connection fee   2,844.
Native Plant Preservation plan 1,375.
Ecological monitoring 500.
Permit fees 6,300.
Impact fee (included in PC Tax)
Other new code compliance estimates 1,500.
New engineering required for IRC code 2,400.
(not required under old UBC code)
The water meter impact fee is scheduled to triple too!

And I am sure I still missed expenses that are buried in our architect/designer's costs in producing the working drawings.

TOTAL REGULATORY COSTS ARE NEARLY 10% OF THE PROJECT AND INCREASING EACH YEAR!

Uncontrolled increase of these fees is a threat to the affordability of housing in our communities, and requires everyone's awareness and involvement to assure responsible control of new and increasing taxes added to new home construction.

WATER PROOFING EXTERIOR AND SITE WALLS

A short note about water proofing is in order, and is very important to your project! Why? Because a wet interior wall, or an exterior wall that has unsightly mineral leeching will impact both the value and maintenance of your home!

Be sure that ALL walls that come in contact with exterior soil, or are in any way exposed to the natural weather elements, include water proofing of some sort. There are an assortment of products that we routinely use, including tar products, Dry lock (tm), Thompson's Water Seal, Behr water sealer, Aqua Seal etc... Each of these products have a place in a project, but be sure you discuss the issue with your builder to assure a complete sealer that is appropriate to the job at hand.

Also, hydrostatic pressure is a structural threat, so you will want to plan for areas where water can accumulate and cause damage by increasing the stress on the structure. Water weighs over 60 pounds per square foot, and the pressure created by the standing water is a function of its depth. In other words, 5 feet of water is equal to over 300 pounds of pressure per square foot (Clark). Allowed to stand for any length of time, this can damage the structure through both pressure and dissolving the surrounding materials.

A simple and inexpensive installation of perforated piping, gravel, and Drylock is often all that is needed to solve the problem. However, **this must be completed during construction** in most cases!

ROOF TYPE AND IMPACT ON CURB APPEAL, COST, AND DURABILITY

Roofing is most often determined by the architectural style you choose for your home, and therefore you will likely be limited in the scope of choices related to design. However, there are several important issues you will want to consider.

Tile roofing is most often in the form of either concrete or clay, and is installed over an already dried in deck (roofing that provides a water tight seal under the tile). The material used below the tile is often hot tar combined with rolled fiberglass, and this is an acceptable method of installation that meets current code and industry standards. We suggest an additional standard due to the fact that the hot tar and fiberglass surface usually has a warranty of less than five years, while the concrete or clay tile has a typical longevity of around thirty years. There are newer products that do cost more to install, but they offer an improved warranty and life expectancy more consistent with the life of the tile (JEV). In addition, there are various ways to install the sub-surface (dried in decking under the tile) which can improve the seal and life of the roof. Finally, there are also interesting ways to make the tile look more custom, such as the use of cement between mission clay tile. This typically costs a little more, but looks great and adds to the curb appeal of the roofing system.

One other note on tile roofing. If you like tile, and want this look on your home, you do not necessarily have to design your entire roofing system out of tile. The patios and some of the tiled roofing area can be combined with pitched roofing behind parapet walls to reduce the initial cost of the entire roof. See some of the photos in this publication for examples of this type of design. You can achieve a Mediterranean tile look with arches and tile on the patios and foyer areas, while designing the less expensive built-up roofing in the interior parts of the home. A standard rule of thumb is that tile can often run three to four times as much as a built-up or shingle roofing system, though this varies widely by product choice and regional labor cost.

Finally, parapet walls should be wrapped up over the top (to the front edge of the home) with heavy (usually 90 pound) fiberglass roofing to completely seal your home. Later the lathers will often cover this seal with black paper or side board, but the lathing and side board should not be used to seal the wall from moisture! There are often leaks through stucco, and there is often a misconception that paint and stucco systems are water proof. They typically are not, unless you choose certain more expensive products such as synthetic stucco or paint sealer.

Also, any and all exterior penetrations (places where plumbing, electrical, HVAC, Viga poles, or any other penetration exists, should be flashed and sealed to keep water out! Construction defect issues are in the spotlight, so you will want to make double sure that your home is water tight! This should also include depressed (sunken) shower pans when your floor is concrete, and the use of appropriate materials that either handle the leakage of shower tile grout seams or resists the moisture within industry standards. **Water that is introduced behind walls is never beneficial to the structure, and often causes mold, dry-rot, structure damage, and other problems which are detrimental to the value and marketability of your home!** There are solutions, but why deal with the problem if you can design and build smart and avoid the issue.

A DISCUSSION ON INTERIOR FINISHES AND INTERIOR DECORATING CHOICES

This publication is not intended to be your final source for Interior Decorating information. However, there are some issues you will likely want to consider. Typically your interior atmosphere is enhanced by color coordination between paint, lighting, tile stains, counter tops and window coverings along with other personalized details. Lighting, color, and the texture of materials is very important to achieving the type of atmosphere you were drawn to during your initial wish list phase of your project. So long as your budget allows, I encourage the use of a professional to help you pull together your interior. At the very least you will want to consult the painting, tile, and cabinet professionals to help you make your interior choices, so that you do not spend thousands of dollars on a beautiful pastel tile floor only to find that is does not blend with your expensive granite counter tops.

FIREPLACE INTERIOR FINISHES (ZERO CLEARANCE AND MASONRY)

Fireplaces typically take the form of either a Zero-Clearance fire box installed in the framing or your home, often with some sort of finish to make it look and feel masonry, and complete masonry fireplaces that look and feel much more solid. Your choice of Zero-Clearance does not have to be viewed as less than masonry, if the box is of high quality, and the exterior detail is chosen well. For example: a typical Santa Fe "beehive" fireplace can include lathe and stucco to make it feel like a masonry unit, while providing the energy efficient benefits many fireplace inserts offer. In addition, pre-cast concrete, flagstone, and rock are often used to dress up the exterior of these inserts. (see photos below)

All of this being said, the masonry fireplace is often the choice of custom home clients. What is the price difference? This depends upon style, detail and material choices, but it is typically between three and five times as much as the Zero-Clearance inserts combined with a pleasing detail to make it look more masonry. Note: this is a rule of thumb, and will certainly vary by region and labor conditions.

CHAPTER 4

ONE OF OUR FLOOR PLANS AND THOUGHT PROCESS

The floor plan shown in this example is one of my own designs, that Design Solutions refined, which reflects several goals and objectives:

A)   A split floor plan for privacy at each side of the home, so that visiting guests can enjoy both privacy and a feeling of connection with the hosts. Also, college age children, and aging parents are easily accommodated with a feeling of independence while also feeling the security of family close by. Note the stack washer and dryer unit on the master bedroom side of the home, and full laundry room off the garage.

B)   The foyer offers the a dramatic entrance that is adjacent to the great room, dining room, and library/office, so guests are exposed to the best first impression possible.

C)   The size of this home is modular. In other words, it can be easily transformed into a three bedroom 3300 square foot home, four bedrooms at 3600 square feet, five bedrooms at 3900 square feet, or a sixth sweet or game room at 4300 square feet. All of these changes are easily accomplished due to the modular shape of each bedroom suite and their placement in the floor plan.

D)   Each bedroom is a suite and includes its own private patio, walk-in closet and sitting area! The size of each suite is approximately 14 feet by 17 feet, which easily accommodates king size beds, futons for guests, desks, and sitting area tables.

E)   Very limited hall way square footage! The hall on the left side doubles as the internet desk, which is available to both the kitchen and bedrooms, for bill paying, study etc... The hallway on the right is also small and doubles as a gallery, with niches etc...

F)   The rear patio doors open into closets, which captures the patio space into the living area for outside entertaining during the spring, summer and fall seasons.

There are many more interesting details you may discover while reviewing this floor plan.

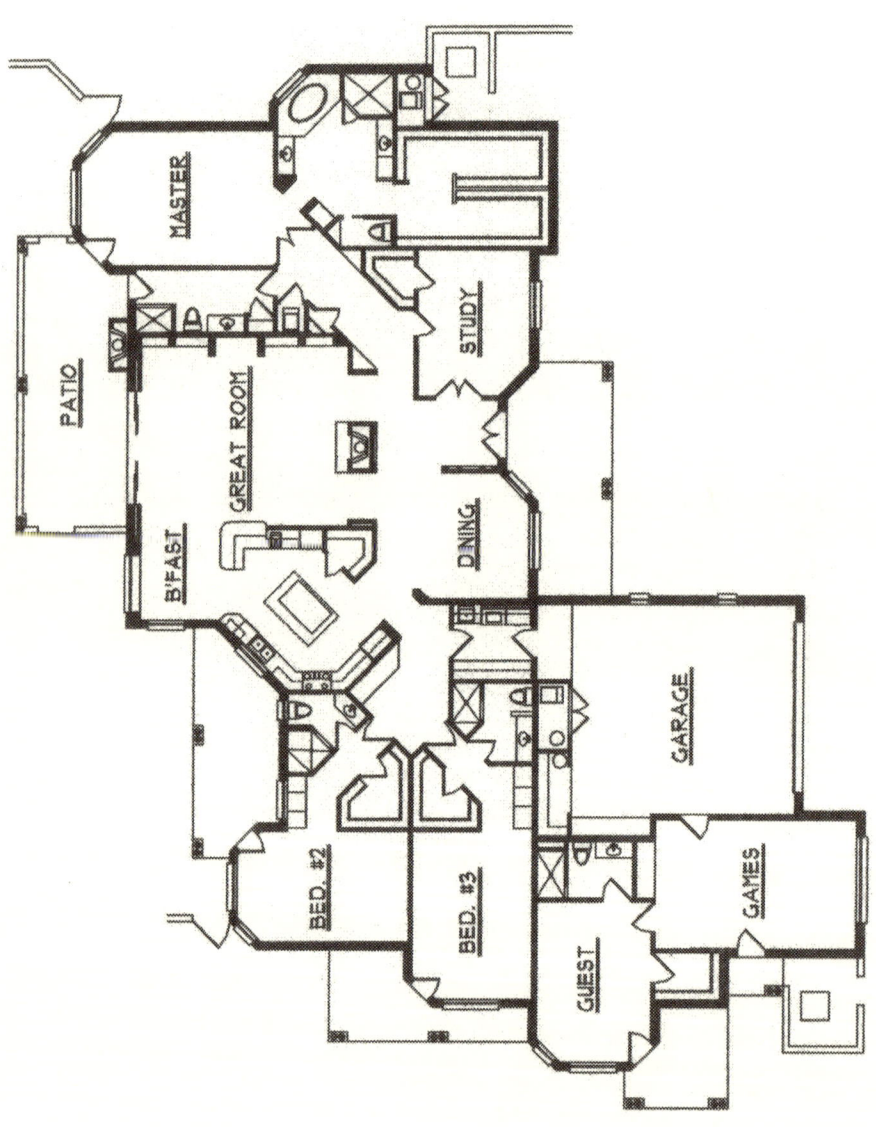

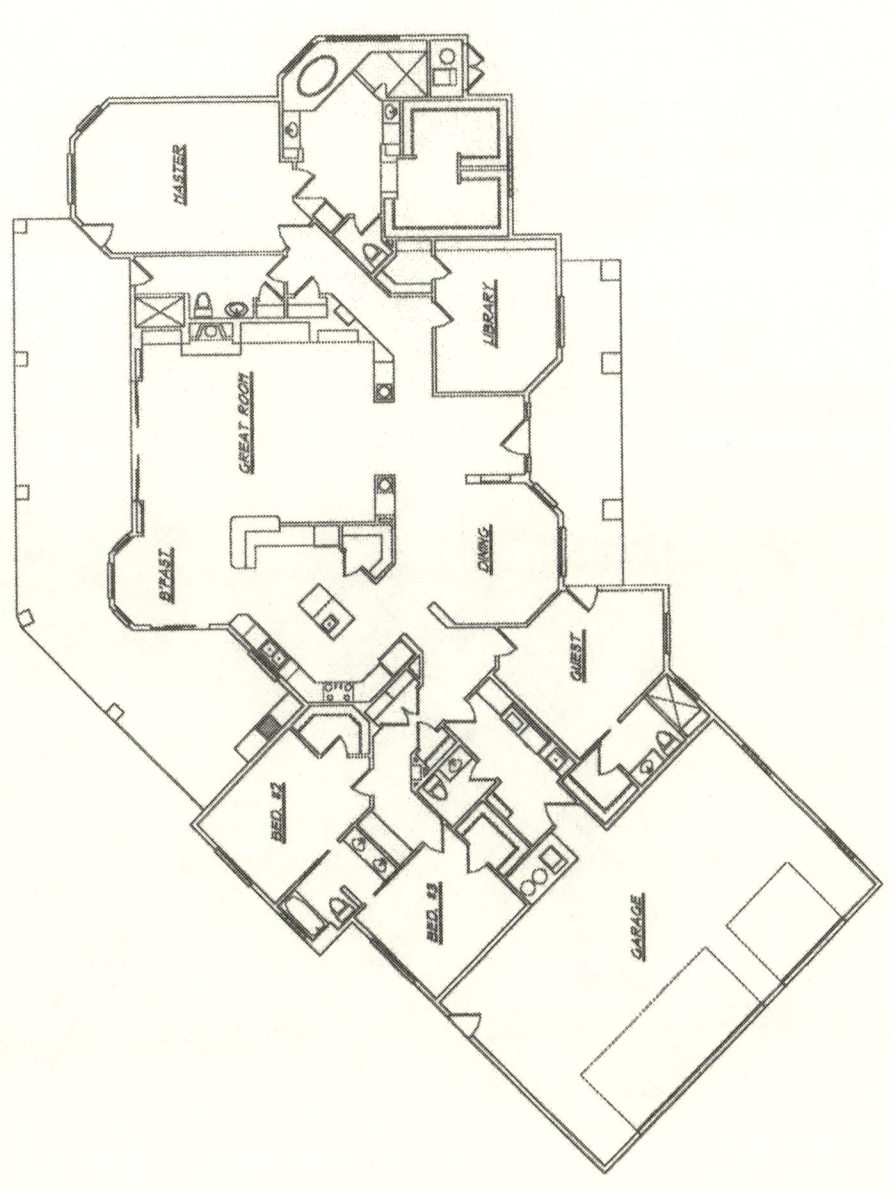

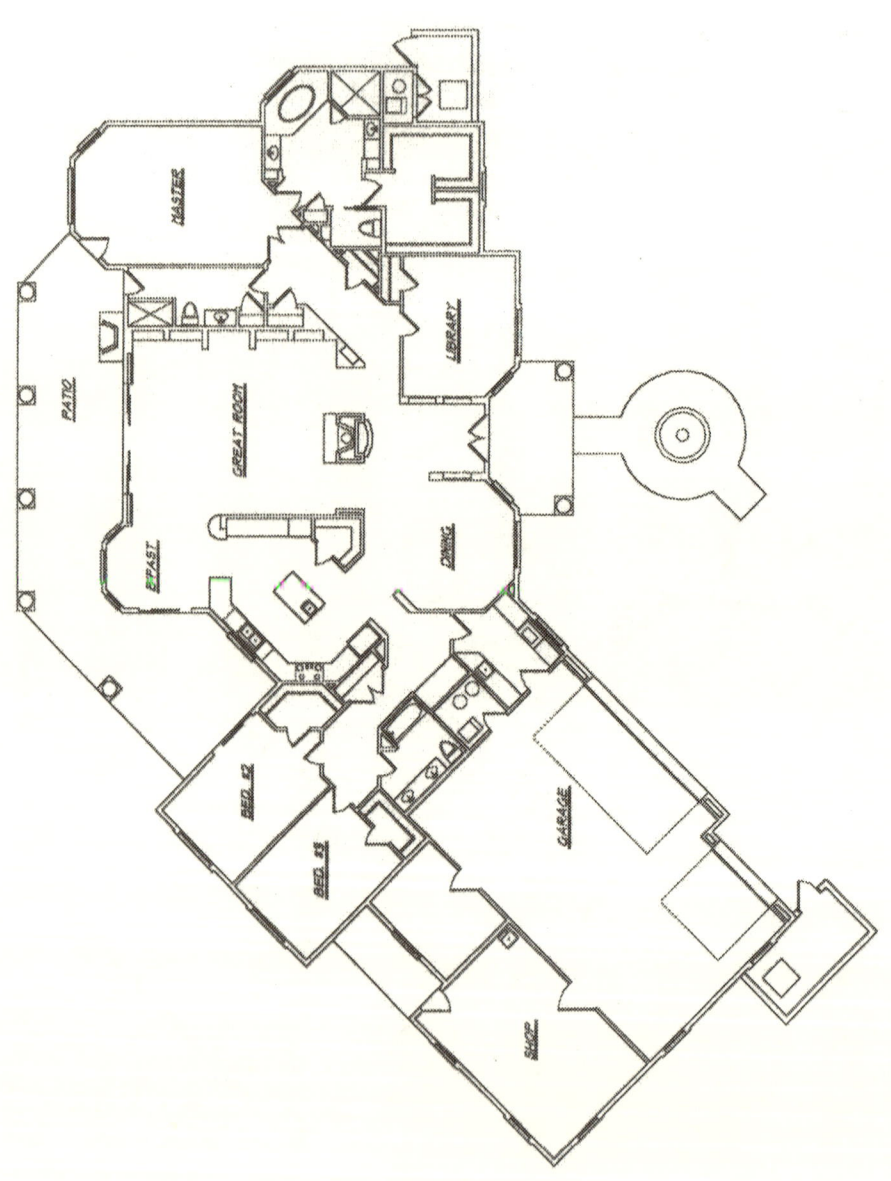

THE ELEVATION AND THOUGHT PROCESS

The exterior elevations on this design are derived from Spanish Colonial influences, yet are very distinctive to the city of Tucson, Arizona. We employ the use of Territorial style parapet walls with a unique repetitive pattern at the top to provide an interesting accent. (to be painted different than the lower wall for accent).

The use of tiled patios, pole and stucco columns, and rough sawn corbelled beams with tongue and groove ceilings helps to add to the southwestern flavor and atmosphere of this design.

Note: This floor plan has been redesigned in Mediterranean, and Santa Fe styles to reflect other owners tastes.

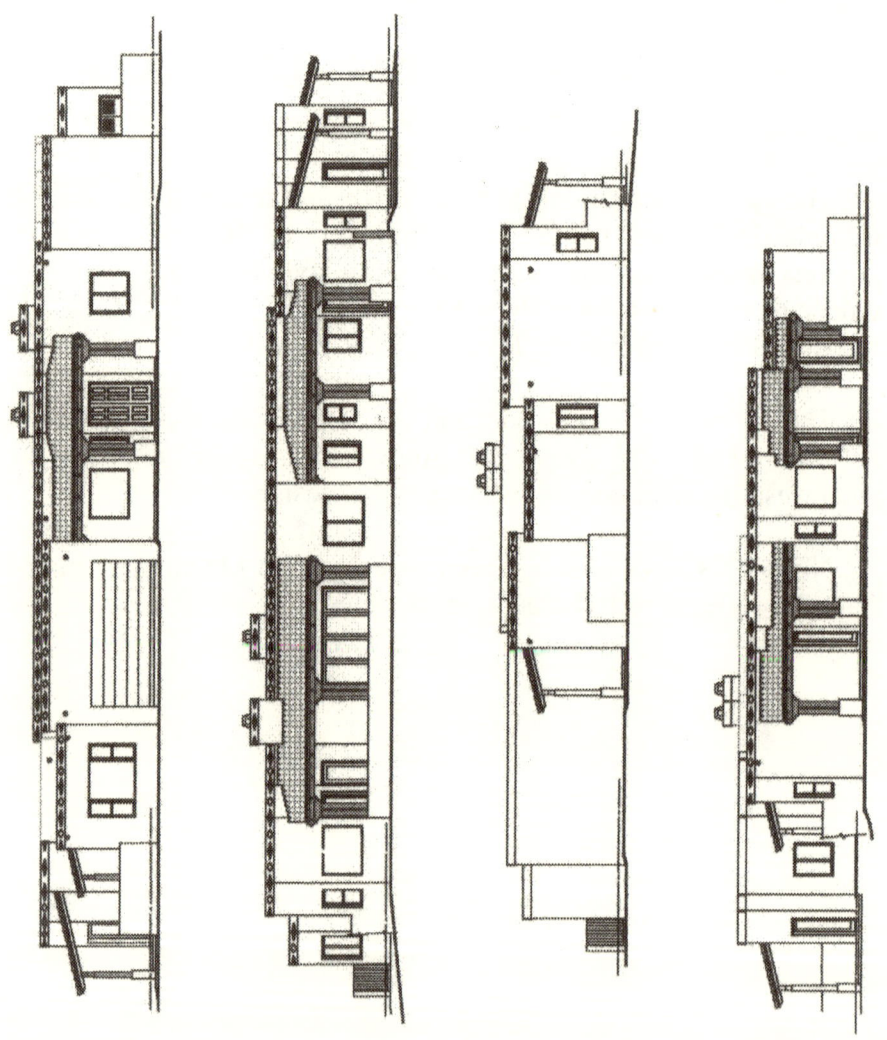

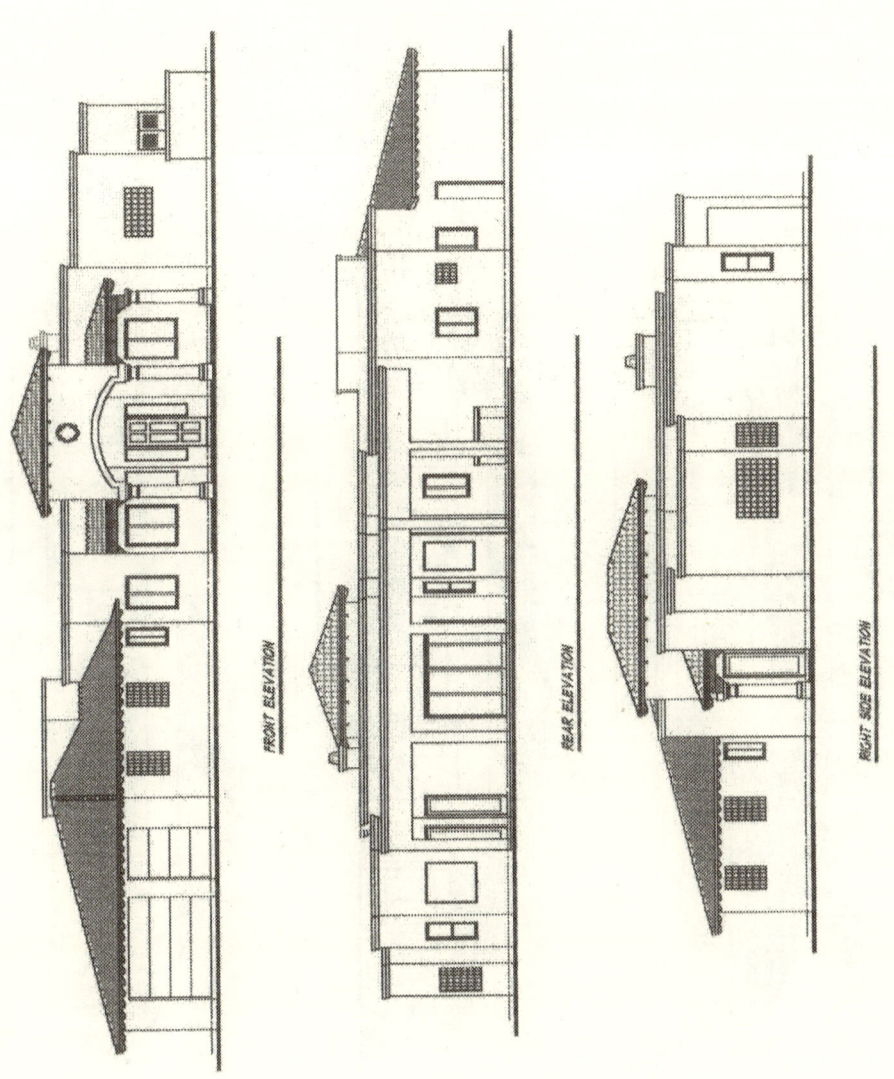

FRONT ELEVATION

REAR ELEVATION

RIGHT SIDE ELEVATION

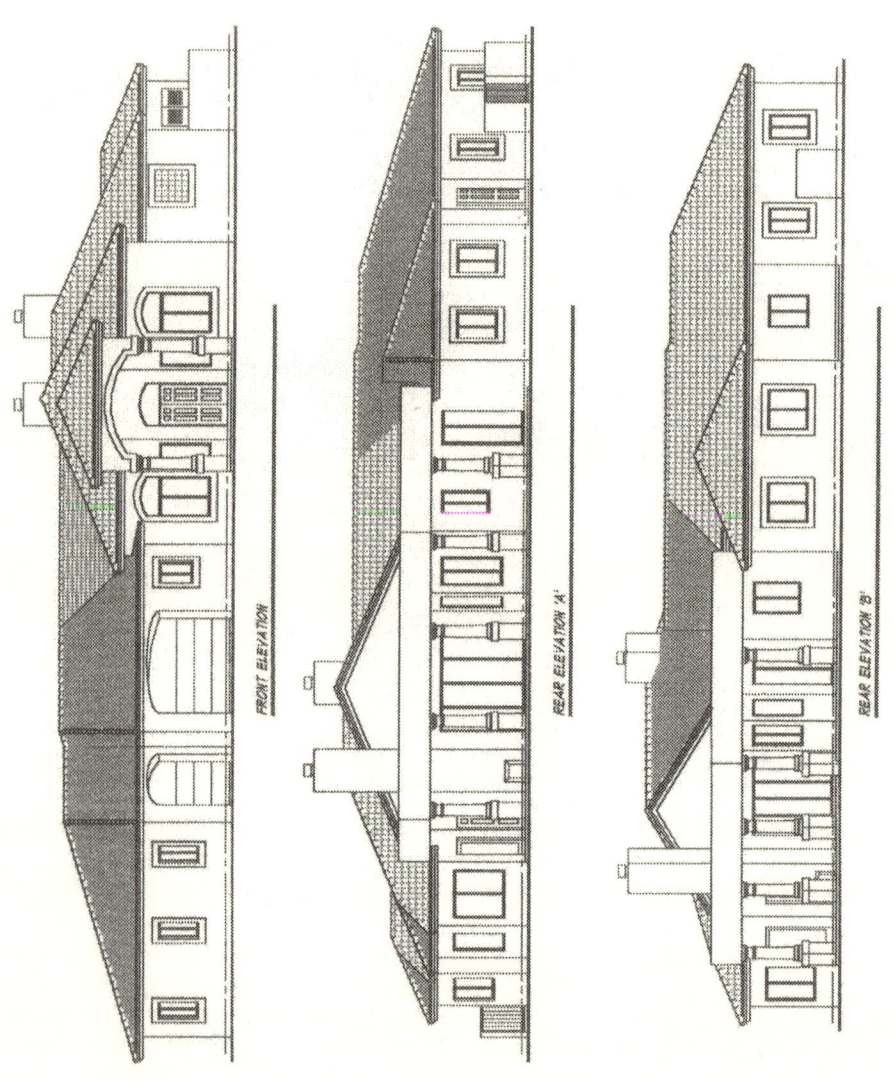

FRONT ELEVATION

REAR ELEVATION 'A'

REAR ELEVATION 'B'

SUMMARY

By now you should have a much better grasp of the step by step designing process that a typical builder uses on each of their projects, assuming you have read the information contained in this book. If the old adage is true, "information is power", then you should now feel much more confident and empowered to begin your own project.

Many industry leaders are not experts in their respective companies, but they generally have basic knowledge of the tasks that each of their associated experts perform on a daily basis. The information you now have should place you in a similar position with regard to your own project. You are not an expert in each area discussed, however, you now have the basic information needed to supervise and direct activity, make important decisions that will affect your home and budget, and to ask specific and knowledgeable questions that you may not have even thought of prior to reviewing the pertinent issues.

Builders, designers/architects, engineers, and owners all bring unique skills and experience to the table, all of which contributes to the success of your project. At the risk of repeating the obvious, your builder is the team quarterback responsible for making your plans and dreams a reality, and therefore is key to the entire project. Keep in mind that the skill of the team assembled contributes to the overall success of your project, and there is a significant difference between price and cost! Skilled experts with the knowledge and experience to complete your project will often not be the lowest initial price (low bid), but they are most often the lowest cost in the end. Mistakes can be avoided, stress can be reduced, and your life can be more enjoyable if you hire the right team of professionals and then use their talents to successfully complete your project.

I have seen and learned from many significant mistakes in the building industry over the years. Foundations installed incorrectly, water proofing issues botched leading to multi-million dollar mistakes, failures to plan for on-site water seepage (natural springs), inadequate water wells, failure to sufficiently plan for future termite and pest re-treatment, and many more issues that you are much less likely to encounter when you employ the services of skilled and experienced members of your team. Mistakes can and do still occur, but they are much less frequent and severe when you rely on experienced individuals.

Your next steps will very likely be to begin looking for the appropriate professionals to help you through your design and building process. Depending upon the phase your are now in, this may require a real estate expert or builder, or possibly both. In either case, you may also want to review some of the basic economics of designing and building your project. A review of these issues is available in our **The American Dream! Building Your Home and Wealth! What the Smart Money Already Knows, publication (ISBN #1-4107-0953-1)** Land selection formulas and building budgets are key components in this publication and can help stack the deck in your favor with regard to an improved home equity position when your project is complete. As with this book, it is designed to help empower you with secrets used by builders daily and basic knowledge you can use to improve your chances of success while reducing your stress.

REFERENCES

2/10 Warranty Program, Tucson, AZ

Abernathy, Scott, Concrete

Barraza, Mark and Lucy and Hansen, Dennis, Diamond Ventures, Tucson, Arizona

Buena, Ramses, Architecture

Clark, Dr. Robert A, Hydrology and Water Resources, University of Arizona, Harshbarger 228 Building Tucson, Arizona

Copplestone, Trewin 2001, Frank Lloyd Wright, A Retrospective View, TODTRI Book Publishers 254 W. 31st Street New York, NY 10001-2813

Cummings, Mary, National City Mortgage, Tucson, AZ

Diamond Ventures Real Estate Development, Tucson, AZ

Fielding, Gavin, Hydrology and Water Resources, University of Arizona, Harshbarger 228 Tucson Arizona

Grenier Engineering Company, Tucson, AZ

Hamstra, Jeff, Hamstra Heating and Air Conditioning, Tucson, AZ

Latham, Hannis, Quad-Lock and Radiant Heat Barrier Supply Companies, Tucson, AZ

Nathanson, Jerry A, 2000, Basic Environmental Technology, Water Supply, Waste Management, and Pollution Control, Third Edition, Prentice Hall Publishing, Upper Saddle River, New Jersey; Columbus Ohio

Nash, Jeff, Koedecker and Kenyon Stucco Company

Nichols, Lanny, Nichols on-site Engineering Company, Tucson, AZ

O'Shaunesy, Sam, Termitinator Company, Tucson, AZ

Pitts, Jim, Design Solutions, 3502 E. Grant Road, Tucson, Arizona

Robles, Al, Handcrafted Tile Company, Tucson, Arizona

Rodriguez, Mariano, MAR Architects, Tucson, Arizona

Salazar, Paul, Excavation

Security Pest Control, Tucson, AZ

Southwest Gas Energy Advantage Plus building program, Tucson, AZ

TEP, Tucson Electric and Power Company's Sun-Share program

Washburn, Steven M 2002, What the Smart Money Already Knows, Designing and Building Custom Homes, and Your Wealth, From a Custom Builders Perspective, First Library Publishing

ABOUT THE AUTHOR

Steven M. Washburn is a SAHBA Certified Custom Builder in Arizona, with experience working in both residential and commercial projects dating back to 1973. His portfolio of successful projects include some of the finest homes on some of the most difficult hillside and rock sites that the southwest has to offer. Washburn Custom Builder's projects have been featured in Southern Arizona Home Builder's Magazine, Arizona Daily Star, Foothills Today, and Tucson Lifestyle Magazine. Steven's early experience includes hands-on sub-contractor experience with the trades that actually construct projects dating back to his teenage years in construction, and he designed and built his first large custom home in 1987. Since then, Steven has been known for building homes with creative design on very difficult sites while maintaining high quality and keeping costs under control.

Steven's educational background includes numerous industry specific courses along with a University of Arizona Bachelor of Arts in Latin American Studies coupled with an International Business Certificate from the University of Arizona Eller College of Business and a minor in Business Administration, with an emphasis on environmental issues and the Spanish language. He has also received the Southern Arizona Home Builder's Association Certified Custom Builder Award. In addition, you will often find him both speaking at and attending various industry seminars and symposiums designed to stay up-to-date in current issues affecting the building business and its clients. (see appendix for more)

Bachelor of Arts from the University of Arizona

Majors: Latin American Studies
International Business Certificate from the University of Arizona
Eller College of Business, Economics Department

Minors: General Business Administration with an emphasis on
Spanish and Hydrology & Water Resources

Industry specific, economic, and tax law courses from The
American College of Oxford and Pima College.
On the board (and team leader) of Agua Prieta Family Shelters Inc, a
non-profit corporation dedicated to building "casita" adobe "ladrillo"
shelters along the US-Mexican border.

Pima County Advisory Committee to the State of Arizona
Department of Environmental Quality
SAHBA Technical Committee, specializing in Septic System and
environmental/water issues.

Historical board, committee positions and affiliations:

Palisades South Architectural Committee Chairman

Tierra Serena Architectural Committee Chairman

Fund raising and construction committee for Immaculate Heart Middle School

MORE ABOUT THE AUTHOR

My wife and I have a dear friend and author, Adrianne, who I asked to proof read this book. She said "There is something missing", speaking of my philosophy and the force to which I subscribe each day. In other words, how does a fifteen year old parent, with both hands tied behind his back from the start, evolve into a successful builder, husband, parent, and any number of hats I choose to wear each day? The answer is both simple and complex.

The simple part is that By the Grace of God I have the talents, blessings, and motivation I use each day to diligently do that which the Lord our God calls each of us to do. I believe it is best said in the Biblical Parable of the Three Servants (Matthew 25:14). Each being given his appropriate allotment of talents, according to their skills, were told to use them wisely in their master's absence. The two that did profited handsomely, and they were rewarded by the master upon his return. They were certainly afraid of failure and loss, but overcame their fear, armed with faith, and ventured out with resulting success. The third servant was timid and had little faith and much fear. He only protected his allotment of talents, and he was dealt with severely for wasting his opportunity and resources.

The message I receive from this parable is to venture out and use my talents on a daily basis, face my fear of failure armed with faith in God's word, and work the talents God has given me. **Knowledge, skills, and talents (resources) that sit idle are of no use at all. It is only when those assets are used that they produce fruit!**

For me, this is only the beginning. There are many more stories and books in the Bible which provide me with direction for my life. This includes how to handle our gains and share our talents and success. We are called to be funnels with our resources, and not dams, meaning that the rewards from our blessings are to be shared with others in need, and thus become seeds that are sown for future harvest (often by and for others). I have been blessed with talents and resources, and I choose to answer God's calling to share my time, talents, and money. I have learned that I always receive far more than I give!

For example: I spent three years working on a committee to raise funds to build the 15,000 square foot Immaculate Heart Middle School, and another year intimately involved with the construction committee. I was in the trenches with the architect, school administration, and workers involved in the design and construction of improvements that required expensive engineering and careful oversight of both design and budget. No sooner than the project was finished I was faced with taking over a failing project (by another builder) that required these very same skills, that I did not have before. This project was successfully built and is now one of my featured success stories. My success is based in my work and experience as an un-paid volunteer answering God's calling to share.

I can cite many such cases over the years, and I have always been blessed with much more than I give in any charitable project.

So what is the complex part of my philosophy answer? It is much shorter and different than you might think.

I am afflicted with being human, so I do not always choose the correct path of action. Today, I am enjoying success beyond anything I could have imagined as a young man starting out in the world. I know this is due to my connection and obedience to God's word. There have been periods of rapid growth and success in my life, and each of them is directly connected with my submission and obedience to His word. Management classes often teach students that to be a good leader you must first be a good follower. This is certainly the case for me, especially where my faith is concerned. There have also been periods of failure and trouble in my life, when I was less than diligent in my pursuit of God's word and direction. My faith and willingness to listen to, and act on, God's direction in my life is the most important factor in my success!

I'll bet you thought I would expound on my own talents, organizational, and building strategies. All of these came after.

As a result of the above, I have also developed several basic business strategies that have contributed to our success.

BUSINESS PHILOSOPHY

1) We are successful when we help our clients achieve success. Designing and building quality projects that reflect the owner's wishes and that contributes to their net worth is essential to our own success.

2) Work daily to keep expenses down and quality high! Also, offer helpful suggestions that improve the project, save expenses, add to the quality, and enhance architectural appeal.

3) Explain and educate clients as to their options and how their choices will impact their project. (Cost, timing, quality, etc…)

4) Listen to the experts! We do not and cannot know it all, so we must ask and listen to the experts in each field. Owners, architects, engineers and sub-contractors are examples of a few of the people we must include in this daily exercise.

5) Last but not least: Integrity in all of our dealings. Respect our clients, sub-contractors, suppliers, and anyone involved with our mission of designing and building Dream Homes or any other project!

www.ingramcontent.com/pod-product-compliance
Lightning Source LLC
Chambersburg PA
CBHW021544290526
45785CB00004BA/1502